INTELLIGENCE AND COUNTERINTELLIGENCE STUDIES

CONTRACTORS IN THE CIVILIAN INTELLIGENCE COMMUNITY

AN ASSESSMENT OF THEIR USE

INTELLIGENCE AND COUNTERINTELLIGENCE STUDIES

Additional books in this series can be found on Nova's website under the Series tab.

Additional e-books in this series can be found on Nova's website under the e-book tab.

INTELLIGENCE AND COUNTERINTELLIGENCE STUDIES

CONTRACTORS IN THE CIVILIAN INTELLIGENCE COMMUNITY

AN ASSESSMENT OF THEIR USE

MAXWELL GIBBS
EDITOR

New York

Copyright © 2014 by Nova Science Publishers, Inc.

All rights reserved. No part of this book may be reproduced, stored in a retrieval system or transmitted in any form or by any means: electronic, electrostatic, magnetic, tape, mechanical photocopying, recording or otherwise without the written permission of the Publisher.

For permission to use material from this book please contact us:
Telephone 631-231-7269; Fax 631-231-8175
Web Site: http://www.novapublishers.com

NOTICE TO THE READER

The Publisher has taken reasonable care in the preparation of this book, but makes no expressed or implied warranty of any kind and assumes no responsibility for any errors or omissions. No liability is assumed for incidental or consequential damages in connection with or arising out of information contained in this book. The Publisher shall not be liable for any special, consequential, or exemplary damages resulting, in whole or in part, from the readers' use of, or reliance upon, this material. Any parts of this book based on government reports are so indicated and copyright is claimed for those parts to the extent applicable to compilations of such works.

Independent verification should be sought for any data, advice or recommendations contained in this book. In addition, no responsibility is assumed by the publisher for any injury and/or damage to persons or property arising from any methods, products, instructions, ideas or otherwise contained in this publication.

This publication is designed to provide accurate and authoritative information with regard to the subject matter covered herein. It is sold with the clear understanding that the Publisher is not engaged in rendering legal or any other professional services. If legal or any other expert assistance is required, the services of a competent person should be sought. FROM A DECLARATION OF PARTICIPANTS JOINTLY ADOPTED BY A COMMITTEE OF THE AMERICAN BAR ASSOCIATION AND A COMMITTEE OF PUBLISHERS.

Additional color graphics may be available in the e-book version of this book.

LIBRARY OF CONGRESS CATALOGING-IN-PUBLICATION DATA

ISBN: 978-1-63321-160-5

Published by Nova Science Publishers, Inc. † New York

CONTENTS

Preface vii

Chapter 1 Civilian Intelligence Community: Additional Actions Needed to Improve Reporting on and Planning for the Use of Contract Personnel 1
United States Government Accountability Office

Chapter 2 Statement of Stephanie O'Sullivan, Principal Deputy Director, Office of the Director of National Intelligence. Hearing on " The Intelligence Community: Keeping Watch Over Its Contractor Workforce" 53

Index 63

PREFACE

This book examines the extent to which the eight civilian IC elements use core contract personnel; the functions performed by these personnel and the reasons for their use; and whether the elements developed policies and strategically planned for their use. GAO reviewed and assessed the reliability of the eight civilian IC elements' core contract personnel inventory data for fiscal years 2010 and 2011, including reviewing a sample of 287 contract records.

Chapter 1 – The IC uses core contract personnel to augment its workforce. These contractors typically work alongside government personnel and perform staff-like work. Some core contract personnel require enhanced oversight because they perform services that could inappropriately influence the government's decision making.

This report is an unclassified version of a classified report issued in September 2013. GAO was asked to examine the eight civilian IC elements' use of contractors.

This report examines (1) the extent to which the eight civilian IC elements use core contract personnel, (2) the functions performed by these personnel and the reasons for their use, and (3) whether the elements developed policies and strategically planned for their use. GAO reviewed and assessed the reliability of the eight civilian IC elements' core contract personnel inventory data for fiscal years 2010 and 2011, including reviewing a sample of 287 contract records.

This sample is nongeneralizable as certain contract records were removed due to sensitivity concerns. GAO also reviewed agency acquisition policies and workforce plans and interviewed agency officials.

Chapter 2 – This is the Statement of Stephanie O'Sullivan, Principal Deputy Director, Office of the Director of National Intelligence. Hearing on "'The Intelligence Community: Keeping Watch Over Its Contractor Workforce.'"

In: Contractors in the Civilian Intelligence ... ISBN: 978-1-63321-160-5
Editor: Maxwell Gibbs © 2014 Nova Science Publishers, Inc.

Chapter 1

CIVILIAN INTELLIGENCE COMMUNITY: ADDITIONAL ACTIONS NEEDED TO IMPROVE REPORTING ON AND PLANNING FOR THE USE OF CONTRACT PERSONNEL[*]

United States Government Accountability Office

WHY GAO DID THIS STUDY

The IC uses core contract personnel to augment its workforce. These contractors typically work alongside government personnel and perform staff-like work. Some core contract personnel require enhanced oversight because they perform services that could inappropriately influence the government's decision making.

This report is an unclassified version of a classified report issued in September 2013. GAO was asked to examine the eight civilian IC elements' use of contractors. This report examines (1) the extent to which the eight civilian IC elements use core contract personnel, (2) the functions performed by these personnel and the reasons for their use, and (3) whether the elements developed policies and strategically planned for their use. GAO reviewed and assessed the reliability of the eight civilian IC elements' core contract personnel inventory data for fiscal years 2010 and 2011, including reviewing a

---

[*] This is an edited, reformatted and augmented version of the United States Government Accountability Office publication, GAO-14-204, dated January 2014.

sample of 287 contract records. This sample is nongeneralizable as certain contract records were removed due to sensitivity concerns. GAO also reviewed agency acquisition policies and workforce plans and interviewed agency officials.

WHAT GAO RECOMMENDS

GAO is recommending that IC CHCO take several actions to improve the inventory data's reliability and transparency and revise strategic workforce planning guidance, and develop ways to identify contracts for services that could affect the government's decision-making authority. IC CHCO generally agreed with GAO's recommendations.

WHAT GAO FOUND

Limitations in the intelligence community's (IC) inventory of contract personnel hinder the ability to determine the extent to which the eight civilian IC elements— the Central Intelligence Agency (CIA), Office of the Director of National Intelligence (ODNI), and six components within the Departments of Energy, Homeland Security, Justice, State, and the Treasury—use these personnel. The IC Chief Human Capital Officer (CHCO) conducts an annual inventory of core contract personnel that includes information on the number and costs of these personnel. However, GAO identified a number of limitations in the inventory that collectively limit the comparability, accuracy, and consistency of the information reported by the civilian IC elements as a whole. For example, changes to the definition of core contract personnel and data shortcomings limit the comparability of the information over time. In addition, the civilian IC elements used various methods to calculate the number of contract personnel and did not maintain documentation to validate the number of personnel reported for 37 percent of the 287 records GAO reviewed. Further, IC CHCO did not fully disclose the effects of such limitations when reporting contract personnel and cost information to Congress, which limits its transparency and usefulness.

The civilian IC elements used core contract personnel to perform a broad range of functions, such as information technology and program management, and reported in the core contract personnel inventory on the reasons for using these personnel. However, limitations in the information on the number and cost of core contract personnel preclude the information on contractor functions from being used to determine the number of personnel and their costs associated with each function. Further, civilian IC elements reported in the inventory a number of reasons for using core contract personnel, such as the need for unique expertise, but GAO found that 40 percent of the contract records reviewed did not contain evidence to support the reasons reported.

Collectively, CIA, ODNI, and the departments responsible for developing policies to address risks related to contractors for the other six civilian IC elements have made limited progress in developing those policies, and the civilian IC elements have generally not developed strategic workforce plans that address contractor use. Only the Departments of Homeland Security and State have issued policies that generally address all of the Office of Federal Procurement Policy's requirements related to contracting for services that could affect the government's decision-making authority. In addition, IC CHCO requires the elements to conduct strategic workforce planning but does not require the elements to determine the appropriate mix of government and contract personnel. Further, the elements' ability to use the core contract personnel inventory as a strategic planning tool is hindered because the inventory does not provide insight into the functions performed by contractors, in particular those that could inappropriately influence the government's control over its decisions. Without guidance, strategies, and tools related to these types of functions, the eight civilian IC elements may not be well-positioned to identify and manage related risks.

ABBREVIATIONS

CIA	Central Intelligence Agency
DEA NN	Drug Enforcement Administration's Office of National Security Intelligence
DHS I&A	Department of Homeland Security's Office of Intelligence and Analysis
DNI	Director of National Intelligence
DOD	Department of Defense
DOE IN	Department of Energy's Office of Intelligence and Counterintelligence
DOJ	Department of Justice
FAR	Federal Acquisition Regulation

FBI	Federal Bureau of Investigation
FTE	full-time equivalent
IC	intelligence community
IC CHCO	Intelligence Community Chief Human Capital Officer
ICD	intelligence community directive
ODNI	Office of the Director of National Intelligence
OFPP	Office of Federal Procurement Policy
OMB	Office of Management and Budget
State INR	Department of State's Bureau of Intelligence and Research
Treasury OIA	Department of the Treasury's Office of Intelligence and Analysis

January 29, 2014

The Honorable Thomas R. Carper
Chairman
The Honorable Tom Coburn, M.D.
Ranking Member
Committee on Homeland Security and Governmental Affairs
United States Senate

The Honorable Claire McCaskill
Chairman

The Honorable Ron Johnson
Ranking Member
Subcommittee on Financial and Contracting Oversight
Committee on Homeland Security and Governmental Affairs
United States Senate

The Honorable Susan M. Collins
United States Senate

The intelligence community (IC) comprises 17 different organizations, or IC elements, across the federal government. Of these, eight are civilian IC elements—the Central Intelligence Agency (CIA), Department of Homeland Security's Office of Intelligence and Analysis (DHS I&A), Department of

Energy's Office of Intelligence and Counterintelligence (DOE IN), Department of State's Bureau of Intelligence and Research (State INR), Department of the Treasury's Office of Intelligence and Analysis (Treasury OIA), Drug Enforcement Administration's Office of National Security Intelligence (DEA NN), Federal Bureau of Investigation (FBI), and the Office of the Director of National Intelligence (ODNI). Like other federal agencies, these civilian IC elements rely on contractors to meet a variety of mission needs. In a 2013 report on intelligence oversight activities, Congress cited long-standing concerns about the IC's reliance on contractors, which it noted increased dramatically after the terrorist attacks of September 11, 2001. In October 2009, the Director of National Intelligence (DNI), who serves as head of the IC, issued Intelligence Community Directive (ICD) 612 to define and establish IC-wide policy for managing the use of core contract personnel that support intelligence missions. As defined by ICD 612, core contract personnel provide a range of direct technical, managerial, and administrative support functions to IC elements—some of which may directly inform government decisions, such as intelligence collection, processing, and analysis, along with program management. Core contract personnel are distinct from individual contract personnel who produce commodities or provide widely available commercial services such as building security. ICD 612 also states that core contract personnel typically work alongside government personnel, augment the government workforce, and perform staff-like work.

Determining whether services should be performed by federal employees, contract personnel, or a mixture of both is essential to the federal government's effective and efficient use of taxpayers' dollars. Further, while the use of contractors can provide benefits in supporting agency missions, such as flexibility to meet immediate needs and obtain unique expertise, their use can also introduce risks for the government to consider and manage. Federal acquisition regulations state that certain functions government agencies perform, such as setting agency policy and issuing regulations, are inherently governmental and must be performed by federal employees.[1] In some cases, contractors perform functions closely associated with the performance of inherently governmental functions.[2] For example, contractors performing certain intelligence analysis activities may closely support inherently governmental functions. Agencies should give special management attention to contractors performing services that closely support inherently governmental functions to guard against the potential for loss of government control and accountability for mission-related policy and program decisions.[3]

Our prior work has examined reliance on contractors and the mitigation of related risks at the Department of Defense (DOD), DHS, and several other civilian agencies and found that they generally did not fully consider and mitigate risks of acquiring services that may inform government decisions.[4] In this context, you asked us to review the civilian IC elements' reliance on contractors. This report is a public version of the classified report that we provided to you in September 2013, which addressed: (1) the extent to which the eight civilian IC elements rely on core contract personnel; (2) the functions performed by core contract personnel and the factors that contribute to their use; and (3) whether the civilian IC elements have developed policies and guidance and strategically planned for their use of contract personnel to mitigate related risks. ODNI, in consultation with the other civilian IC elements, deemed some of the information in the September 2013 report as classified, which must be protected from public disclosure. Therefore, this report omits sensitive information about (1) the number and associated costs of government and core contract personnel and some details on how the civilian IC elements prepare the core contract personnel inventory, (2) specific contracts from civilian IC elements we reviewed, and (3) details related to the civilian IC elements' or their respective departments' progress in developing policies to mitigate risks related to contractors and the civilian IC elements' strategic workforce planning efforts.

To determine the extent to which the civilian IC elements rely on core contract personnel, the functions performed by these personnel, and the factors that contribute to their use, we requested and reviewed data from each of the eight civilian IC elements: CIA, DEA NN, DHS I&A, DOE IN, FBI, ODNI, State INR, and Treasury OIA.[5] These data submissions were provided by the civilian IC elements to the IC Chief Human Capital Officer (IC CHCO) for use in the annual core contract personnel inventories. We reviewed five data fields related to information on obligations, the number of full-time equivalents (FTE) on core contracts, the functions performed by core contract personnel, and the reasons for using these personnel.

We originally planned to review fiscal years 2007 through 2011 inventory data. However, we could not conduct a reliability assessment of the data for fiscal years 2007 through 2009 due to a variety of factors. These factors include civilian IC element officials' stating that they could not locate records of certain years' submissions or that obtaining the relevant documentation would require an unreasonable amount of time. As a result, we generally focused our review on data from fiscal years 2010 and 2011. To assess the data's reliability, we selected a random nongeneralizable sample of 287 records—representing 222 contracts or purchase orders—and compared the information reported in these elements' submissions for these years to contract documents.[6] Observations from our nongeneralizable sample cannot be used to make projections about the eight civilian IC elements' submissions as a whole.[7] We determined that four of the five data fields we reviewed—fiscal year obligations, total FTEs, reason code, and budget category—were not sufficiently reliable for the purpose of our review. We present these data and their associated limitations where appropriate in the report. The fifth data field, primary contractor occupation and competency expertise, was sufficiently reliable, though we identified some limitations. Appendix II contains a more detailed discussion of our data reliability assessment. We also reviewed relevant IC CHCO guidance and documents and interviewed agency officials responsible for compiling and processing the data.

To determine whether the civilian IC elements have developed policies and guidance and strategically planned for their use of core contract personnel to mitigate related risks, we reviewed relevant acquisition policies and guidance, workforce planning documents, and strategic planning tools. We also interviewed human capital, procurement, or program officials at each civilian IC element to discuss ongoing efforts related to developing policies and strategic planning to mitigate risks. We compared these plans, guidance, and tools to Office of Management and Budget (OMB) guidance that address risks related to contracting for work closely supporting inherently governmental and critical functions, including the Office of Federal Procurement Policy (OFPP) Policy Letter 11-01, OMB's Memorandum on Managing the Multisector Workforce, and OMB's memoranda on service contract inventories.[8] Further, we compared the civilian IC elements' efforts to strategic human capital best practices identified in our prior work.[9]

A detailed description of our scope and methodology is included in appendix I. We conducted this performance audit from November 2012 to September 2013 in accordance with generally accepted government auditing standards. We subsequently worked with ODNI from September 2013 to December 2013 to prepare an unclassified version of this report for public release. Government auditing standards require that we plan and perform the audit to obtain sufficient, appropriate evidence to provide a reasonable basis for our findings and conclusions based on our audit objectives. We believe the evidence obtained provides a reasonable basis for our findings and conclusions based on our audit objectives.

BACKGROUND

Organization of the IC

Established by the Intelligence Reform and Terrorism Prevention Act of 2004, DNI serves as head of the IC, acts as the principal advisor to the President and National Security Council on intelligence matters, and oversees and directs the implementation of the National Intelligence Program.[10] The IC comprises 17 different organizations, or IC elements, across the federal government represented by 6 executive departments. These IC elements include ODNI, seven other civilian IC elements, and nine military IC elements. The eight civilian IC elements within the scope of our review include two intelligence agencies and six intelligence components within five departments (see figure 1).[11] For the purposes of this review, we are referring to the eight as the civilian IC elements. Appendix III provides additional information on each of the eight civilian IC elements' missions.

Source: GAO analysis of ODNI information.

Figure 1. Civilian IC Elements and Their Respective Departments.

IC Core Contract Personnel Inventory

IC CHCO officials indicated they are responsible for leading the design, development, and execution of human resource strategies, plans, and policies for the IC. In this role, IC CHCO works with both the civilian and military IC elements to collect and maintain information on the use of core contract personnel throughout the IC. Since fiscal year 2007, IC CHCO has compiled an annual core contract personnel inventory to provide information to Congress and others about the IC's use of core contract personnel. This effort was in response to concerns from Congress that the IC relied too heavily on contractors and could not account for the number and costs of contract personnel on an annual basis.

The core contract personnel inventory includes information on both the civilian and military IC elements' contracts for over 10 different data fields.[12] IC CHCO uses information from the inventory to develop an annual briefing for Congress, which includes year-to-year changes in the number of and reasons for using core contract personnel across the IC. In addition, since fiscal year 2011, IC CHCO has prepared a statutorily required IC-wide annual personnel level assessment.[13] As part of this assessment, IC CHCO is required, in consultation with all of the IC elements, to report on the current, projected, and prior five fiscal years' number and costs of core contract personnel, as well as present the budget submission for personnel costs for the upcoming fiscal year.

To prepare the inventory, IC CHCO provides guidance and a data call to the IC elements on an annual basis that details how the elements should report information on their core contracts from the previous fiscal year. Civilian IC element officials stated that generally their elements' contracting, program, finance office, or a combination thereof, collects and reports the information for the data call.

Risks Related to Reliance on Core Contract Personnel

For more than 20 years, OMB procurement policy has indicated that agencies should provide a greater degree of scrutiny when contracting for services that can affect the government's decision-making authority.[14] Without proper management and oversight, such services risk inappropriately influencing the government's control over and accountability for decisions that may be supported by contractors' work. The policy therefore directs agencies to ensure that they maintain sufficient government expertise to manage the contracted work. The Federal Acquisition Regulation also addresses the importance of management oversight associated with contractors providing services that have the potential to influence the authority, accountability, and responsibilities of government employees.[15] Core contract personnel perform the types of functions that may affect an IC element's decision- making authority or control of its mission and operations. While core contract personnel may perform functions that closely support inherently governmental work, these personnel are generally prohibited from performing inherently governmental functions, which require discretion in applying government authority or value judgments in making decisions that can only be performed by government employees.[16] Figure 2 illustrates how the risk of contractors influencing government decision making is increased as core contract personnel perform functions that closely support inherently governmental functions.

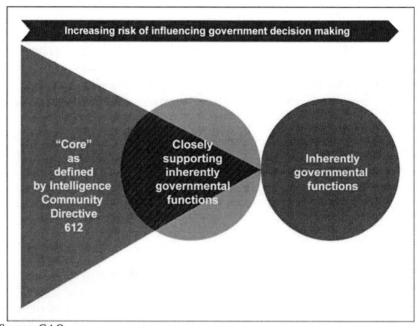

Source: GAO.

Figure 2. Risk Associated with the Use of Core Contract Personnel.

OMB has initiated a number of government-wide interrelated efforts that help to address the risks related to relying on contractors for services that are closely associated with inherently governmental work or critical to an agency's mission (see app. IV for additional information on these OMB policy requirements). Although the IC elements are not required to address certain aspects of the OMB policies, either because of the classified nature of the contracts or because the IC element is a component of an executive department, these efforts provide IC elements with leading practices related to considering and mitigating risks when relying on contractors to perform services that are closely associated with inherently governmental and critical functions. The IC elements are also required to follow applicable IC-wide guidance and federal laws and regulations on the use of contractors. In addition, the departmental elements—the six civilian IC elements that are components within executive departments—must comply with related departmental policies and guidance. For example, DEA NN must comply with federal laws and regulations as well as all applicable OMB, DOJ, DEA, and IC-wide guidance.

OMB's July 2009 guidance and our prior work have emphasized that decisions regarding the use of contractors should be based on strategic workforce planning regarding what types of work are best done by government personnel or by contractors.[17] Specifically, agencies should identify the appropriate mix of government and contract personnel on a function-by-function basis, especially for functions that are critical to an agency's mission. The OMB guidance requires an agency to have sufficient internal capability to control its mission and operations when contracting for these critical functions. Our prior work has found that agencies should have overarching strategic-level guidance related to the extent to which contractors should be used, and agencies' strategic workforce planning documents should contain evidence of strategic considerations of contractor use.[18] In May 2013, we found that DOD had not yet assessed the appropriate mix of government and contract personnel in its strategic workforce plans as required by law and, as a result, was hampered in making more informed strategic workforce decisions. We recommended that DOD revise existing workforce policies and procedures to address the determination of the appropriate workforce mix.[19] DOD partially concurred with this recommendation and noted that it had efforts underway to determine the workforce mix.

OFPP's September 2011 Policy Letter 11-01 builds on past federal policies on closely supporting inherently governmental functions by including a detailed checklist of responsibilities that must be carried out when agencies rely on contractors to perform services that closely support inherently governmental functions. The policy letter also builds upon past OMB guidance by seeking to broaden agencies' focus to include critical functions, which can pose a risk if not carefully monitored. The policy letter establishes criteria agencies are to use in identifying their critical functions, which are functions that are necessary to the agency to effectively perform and maintain control of its mission and operations. The policy letter further states that the more important the function, the more important it is that the agency have internal capability to maintain control of its mission and operations. The policy letter requires executive branch departments and agencies to develop and maintain internal procedures to address the requirements of the guidance.

Further, OFPP's November 2010 and December 2011 guidance on service contract inventories[20] and our prior work[21] have emphasized that an inventory of contracted services, if effectively developed and analyzed, can inform an agency's strategic workforce planning efforts and help identify which contracts may require additional oversight. The inventories can assist an agency in understanding the extent to which contractors are being used to perform activities that closely support inherently governmental work or support the agency's mission and operations. Civilian agencies and DOD are statutorily required to compile service contract inventories on an annual basis.[22] In September 2012, we found that the civilian agencies did not have good visibility on the number of contractor personnel or their role in supporting agency activities because they had not yet collected these data in their fiscal year 2011 inventories.[23]

Additionally, in May 2013, we found that DOD generally continued to have challenges collecting key data in its fiscal year 2011 inventory, which limited the utility, accuracy, and completeness of the inventory data.[24] Specifically, most DOD components, other than the Army, were not able to determine the number of contractor FTEs used to perform each contracted service and were still not able to identify and record more than one type of service purchased for each contracting action entered into the inventory. We made a number of recommendations to help implement and improve both the civilian agencies' and DOD's service contract inventories. For example, we recommended that OMB clarify guidance to require agencies to consistently report on the number of contract personnel. OMB generally concurred with our recommendations and agreed to work with the agencies to strengthen their use of service contract inventories by sharing lessons learned and best practices from the initial inventories.

LIMITATIONS IN THE INVENTORY UNDERMINE ABILITY TO DETERMINE EXTENT OF CIVILIAN IC ELEMENTS' RELIANCE ON CONTRACTORS

Due to limitations in the core contract personnel inventory, we could not accurately determine the extent to which the eight civilian IC elements have used core contract personnel. The inventory contains two data fields—fiscal year obligations and total FTEs—that IC CHCO uses to identify the civilian IC elements' extent of contractor reliance. IC CHCO used this inventory information to report to Congress that from fiscal year 2009 to 2011, the number of core contract personnel for the civilian IC elements declined by approximately 30 percent. However, we identified several issues that limit the comparability, accuracy, and consistency of the information reported by the civilian IC elements as a whole. First, changes to the definition of core contract personnel and data reliability limitations identified by the elements for certain years hinder the ability to use the inventory to make year-to-year comparisons of cost and FTE data. Second, our analysis found that the reported contract costs for the fiscal years 2010 and 2011 inventories were inaccurate or inconsistently determined. Third, elements calculated the number of core contract personnel FTEs differently, affecting the consistency of the information reported. In addition, a lack of readily available documentation limits the civilian IC elements' ability to validate the information reported. Further, IC CHCO did not clearly explain the effect of the limitations when reporting the information to Congress. On an individual basis, some of the limitations we identified may not raise significant concerns. When taken together, however, they undermine the utility of the information for determining and reporting on the extent to which the civilian IC elements use core contract personnel.

Changes to Core Contract Personnel Definition and Data Shortcomings Limit Comparability of Obligation and FTE Data across Years

Trends in the civilian IC elements' use of core contract personnel from fiscal year 2007 to 2011 in terms of the number of personnel and associated costs cannot be identified due to changes in the definition of core contract personnel and known data shortcomings. However, IC CHCO used the inventory information to compare IC-wide core contract personnel use from year to year when reporting to Congress. In response to federal statute, IC CHCO prepares an annual personnel assessment that compares the current and projected number and costs of core contract personnel to the number and costs during the prior 5 years. According to IC CHCO, the number of core contract personnel FTEs and associated costs declined nearly one-third from fiscal year 2009 to fiscal year 2011. However, we could not validate the extent to which there was a change in the number of core contract personnel providing support as we determined that a significant portion of the reported reduction is attributable to definitional changes and improvements to data systems. Further, we assessed the reliability of the civilian IC elements' reported information for the total FTEs and fiscal year obligations data fields and determined that the data were not sufficiently reliable for our purpose of identifying the extent of reliance on core contract personnel (see app. II).

Since IC CHCO's initial data collection efforts for the core contract personnel inventory in fiscal year 2006, it has taken actions to further clarify and refine its guidance to address concerns that IC elements were interpreting the definition of core contract personnel differently and to improve the consistency of the information in the inventory. IC CHCO worked with the elements to develop a standard definition that was formalized with the issuance of ICD 612 in October 2009. Further, IC CHCO formed the IC Core Contract Personnel Inventory Control Board, which has representatives from all of the IC elements, to provide a forum to resolve differences in the interpretation of IC CHCO's guidance for the inventory. As a result of the board's efforts, IC CHCO provided supplemental guidance in fiscal year 2010 to either include or exclude certain contract personnel, such as those performing administrative support, training support, and information technology services. For example, the guidance stated that IC elements should include contract personnel who provide training that is unique to the IC mission but exclude those who provide training commercially available through a vendor. IC CHCO officials told us that changes made over time were intended to clarify the definition of core contract personnel and improve the consistency of the information in the inventory. Appendix V summarizes the major changes in the definition reflected in IC CHCO's guidance from fiscal years 2007 through 2011.

While these changes could improve the inventory data, it is unclear the extent to which the definitional changes contributed to the reported decrease in the number of core contract personnel and associated costs from year to year. For example, for fiscal year 2010, officials from one civilian IC element told us they stopped reporting information technology help desk contractors, which had been previously reported, to be consistent with IC CHCO's revised definition. One of these officials stated consequently that the element's reported reduction in core contract personnel between fiscal years 2009 and 2010 did not reflect an actual change in their use of core contract personnel, but rather a change in how core contract personnel were defined for the purposes of reporting to IC CHCO. The official told us that their reported information for fiscal year 2010 was therefore not comparable to data from prior years, in part because of definitional changes.

Further, this civilian IC element identified data reliability limitations in the information reported to IC CHCO for certain fiscal years' inventories, which the element has taken steps to address. However, while IC CHCO noted that this civilian IC element implemented an enhanced contract management system that affected the element's reporting in the briefing and annual personnel level assessment, IC CHCO did not disclose how these improvements affected the ability to compare data across years. For its submission to the fiscal year 2011 inventory, officials from the civilian IC element stated that they used a new contract management system that provided more clarity into which FTEs and obligations should be included in the inventory and thus improved the reliability of their reported information. These officials acknowledged significant limitations with certain aspects of their reported data prior to fiscal year 2011 due to limitations with the contract management system used for those years. For example, officials told us that prior to the contract system upgrade, the system did not allow them to accurately separate out which obligations and FTEs on certain contracts should be considered core versus non-core. As a result, these officials stated that we should not compare the information reported from fiscal year 2010 to 2011 due to the improvements made in the contract management system.

However, IC CHCO included this civilian IC element's data when calculating the IC's overall reduction in number of core contract personnel between fiscal years 2009 and 2011 in its fiscal year 2011 briefing to Congress. In addition, IC CHCO included these data when comparing the number and costs of core contract personnel between fiscal year 2009 and 2011 in the fiscal year 2013 personnel level assessment. OMB guidelines provide that agencies should ensure that disseminated information be reliable, clear, and useful to the intended users.[25] IC CHCO explained in the briefing and personnel level assessment that this civilian IC element's rebaselining had an effect on the element's reported number of contractor personnel for fiscal year 2010. IC CHCO did not explain that the rebaselining would limit the comparability of the number and costs of core contract personnel for both this civilian IC element and the IC as a whole because the element did not adjust the number and costs previously reported.

In addition, another civilian IC element changed its methodology for calculating core contract personnel FTEs over time, which limits the ability to compare this FTE information across certain years. Prior to its submission to the fiscal year 2010 inventory, this element calculated an estimated number of core contract personnel FTEs by applying a certain percentage to the number of contractor FTEs. For its submissions to the fiscal year 2010 and 2011 inventories, the element reported the actual number of core contract personnel FTEs. According to officials from this civilian IC element, because the methodology for calculating the number of core contract personnel FTEs fundamentally changed from fiscal year 2009 to 2010, the data cannot be compared across these years. However, IC CHCO reported and compared these numbers in its annual briefings and personnel level assessments without including information on these changes and any associated limitations. IC CHCO officials stated that they rely on the IC elements to inform them of any methodological changes that would impact the information reported. In addition, IC CHCO officials stated that they identify any major differences between fiscal years and the associated causes. By not fully disclosing the appropriate qualifications for making year-to-year comparisons, the information reported in the briefings and personnel level assessments may not be consistent with leading practices outlined in OMB's guidelines for disseminated information.

Inventory Does Not Accurately and Consistently Account for Contract Costs

The civilian IC elements' core contract personnel costs for fiscal years 2010 and 2011 could not be reliably determined, in part because our analysis identified numerous discrepancies between the amount of obligations reported by the civilian IC elements in the core contract personnel inventory and these elements' supporting documentation for the records we reviewed. We compared the information reported for a sample of 287 records—representing 222 contracts or purchase orders—from the civilian IC elements' submissions for the fiscal years 2010 and 2011 inventories. We found that the civilian IC elements either under- or over-reported the amount of obligations by more than 10 percent for approximately one-fifth of the records. In addition, the civilian IC elements could not provide complete documentation to validate the information reported for 17 percent of the records we reviewed. Overall, we were able to validate the amount of reported obligations for approximately 43 to 77 percent of the records we reviewed at any one element. However, IC CHCO used the core contract personnel inventory information to report fiscal years 2010 and 2011 contract costs for the eight civilian IC elements in our review.

Civilian IC element officials identified several issues that may account for the discrepancies between the reported obligations and the documentation provided. For example, ODNI officials told us that the system used to report their fiscal year 2010 data had reliability issues, in part because the users had to manually enter obligations for certain contracts or manually delete duplicate contracts to avoid double-counting obligations. ODNI officials stated that a new contract management system was used for reporting contract obligations in their submission for the fiscal year 2011 inventory. According to these officials, the new system offers greater detail and improved functionality for identifying the amount of obligations on their contracts. While we observed an improvement in ODNI's reporting of obligations from fiscal year 2010 to 2011, we still identified discrepancies in 18 percent of ODNI's fiscal year 2011 records in our sample. ODNI officials noted that, even with the new system, they manually enter the information into the inventory submission, which may result in data entry errors.

Internal control activities, such as accurate and timely recording of transactions, help provide reasonable assurance of the reliability of reported information. According to federal internal control standards, for an agency to run and control its operations, it must have relevant, reliable information relating to internal events.[26] IC CHCO officials stated that they review the IC elements' submissions for outliers and obvious errors but rely on the elements to ensure the accuracy of the information, in part because IC CHCO does not have the staff resources for more extensive reviews. IC CHCO officials also explained that their role is to provide guidance to the IC elements for reporting the information to the inventory but not to audit the reliability of the information reported. While civilian IC element officials described some steps taken to help ensure the reliability of the information reported, such as reviewing the information reported for outliers or prohibiting changes without prior approval, these internal controls may not be sufficient in light of the challenges we identified.

In addition, we found that the reported costs in the inventory, which support the personnel level assessments and briefings to Congress, may not fully account for the amount of obligations on certain core contracts in a given fiscal year based on the methods permitted by IC CHCO guidance. IC CHCO's guidance for the fiscal years 2010 and 2011 inventories generally requires IC elements to report on the total amount of funds obligated to contracts during the fiscal year. However, the guidance also indicates that reporting on a snapshot of active contracts on September 30 is an acceptable method for the large elements. This practice may lead to elements not fully accounting for the amount of obligations within a fiscal year on contracts. For example, officials from two civilian IC elements told us they do not report the amount of obligations on contracts or contract line items that are no longer active as of September 30.[27] Officials acknowledged that in some cases, obligations may not be reported as a result of the exclusion of inactive contracts or contract option periods. However, IC CHCO does not disclose this methodology or its effects on the information it reports to Congress.

Lack of Detailed Guidance and Complete Documentation Limit Consistency of FTE Information Reported

The number of core contract personnel providing support to the civilian IC elements for fiscal years 2010 and 2011 could not be reliably determined, in part because we found that the eight civilian IC elements used significantly different methodologies when determining the number of FTEs. For example, some civilian IC elements estimated contract personnel FTEs using target labor hours while other civilian IC elements calculated the number of FTEs using the labor hours invoiced by the contractor. As a result, the reported numbers are not comparable across these elements. The IC CHCO core contract personnel inventory guidance for both fiscal years 2010 and 2011 state that full accounting is the preferred method for identifying FTEs, but does not provide additional detail, such as specifying appropriate methodologies for calculating FTEs, requiring IC elements to describe their methodologies, or requiring IC elements to disclose any associated limitations with their methodologies.

Depending on the methodology used, an element can calculate a different number of FTEs for the same contract. For example, for one contract we reviewed at a civilian IC element that reports FTEs based on actual labor hours invoiced by the contractor, the element reported 16 FTEs for the contract. For the same contract, however, a civilian IC element that uses estimated labor hours at the time of award would have calculated 27 FTEs. As a result, using different methodologies limits the comparability of civilian IC elements' reported numbers and obscures what the information represents in a given fiscal year. IC CHCO officials stated they have discussed standardizing the methodology for calculating the number of FTEs with the IC elements but identified challenges, such as identifying a standard labor-hour conversion factor for one FTE. IC CHCO guidance for fiscal year 2012 instructs elements to provide the total number of direct labor hours worked by the contract personnel to calculate the number of FTEs for each contract, as opposed to allowing for estimates, which could improve the consistency of the FTE information reported across the IC. Since this methodology is different than the methodology used by several civilian IC elements to calculate their number of FTEs in the fiscal year 2010 and 2011 inventories, IC CHCO will be further limited in the extent to which it can compare FTE data across years.

In addition, we found that most of the civilian IC elements did not maintain readily available documentation of the information used to calculate the number of FTEs reported for a significant number of the records we reviewed. As a result, these elements could not easily replicate the process for calculating or validate the reliability of the information reported for these records. Federal internal control standards call for appropriate documentation to help ensure the reliability of the information reported.[28] For 37 percent of the 287 records we reviewed, we could not determine the reliability of the information reported. Two of the civilian IC elements were able to provide documentation to support the number of FTEs reported for almost all of the records we reviewed, but the other civilian IC elements experienced challenges in providing documentation to varying degrees. For example, officials from one civilian IC element explained that they did not document how they calculated the number of core contract personnel FTEs at the time of reporting. As a result, these officials stated that it would be very time-consuming to replicate the process for making these calculations, and that, for contracts with higher numbers of contract personnel, it could take months to recreate the methodology used. In addition, another civilian IC element had challenges providing documentation for certain records, in part because some contracts included in the inventory are fixed-price contracts for which it does not negotiate or have insight into the number of FTEs. While IC CHCO does not require the IC elements to maintain documentation of their calculations, without complete documentation, elements cannot ensure the reliability of the information reported in their submissions or may not be able to replicate the methodology used to report the number of FTEs for their contracts. However, IC CHCO aggregates and compares the FTE data across the civilian IC elements when reporting to Congress and has not disclosed in its briefings or personnel level assessments that the FTEs, reported collectively or by element, reflect various definitions and methods of counting contract personnel.

IC CHCO and the civilian IC element officials further identified several challenges related to elements' preparation of their inventory submissions. Officials at several civilian IC elements stated that they experienced turnover in the staff who prepared their submissions over the years. As a result, these officials were unable to explain the methodology used by staff to report the information for certain submissions in prior years. IC CHCO officials stated that they frequently have to work with new staff at the elements to help them understand the reporting requirements because the elements did not have documentation of how prior staff reported certain information. In addition, for a large civilian IC element, many contracting and program officials can be involved in preparing the elements' submissions, making it difficult to ensure consistency in reporting.

INVENTORY PROVIDES LIMITED INSIGHT INTO FUNCTIONS PERFORMED BY CONTRACTORS AND REASONS FOR THEIR USE

The civilian IC elements have used core contract personnel to perform a range of functions, such as human capital, information technology, and program management, and have reported in the core contract personnel inventory the reasons for using contractors for such functions. Due to limitations in the core contract personnel inventory, the number of core contract personnel performing these functions in support of the civilian IC elements and the reasons for their use cannot be reliably determined. We found for the contracts we reviewed, the civilian IC elements generally reported reliable information in the inventory on functions performed by contractors by selecting from one of over 20 broad categories. However, the limitations we identified in the inventory's obligation and FTE data preclude the information on contractor functions from being used to determine the extent to which civilian IC elements contracted for each function. Further, in the inventory, the civilian IC elements provided information on their reasons for using core contract personnel, such as the need for unique expertise, but our analysis found that 40 percent of the contracts in our sample did not contain evidence of the reasons reported. As a result, we could not corroborate the information reported in the inventory on the reasons for using core contract personnel. Moreover, the most widely cited reason in the sample of contracts we reviewed does not describe why a civilian IC element contracted for a service but rather describes the nature of the contract.

Extent to Which Functions Are Performed by Contract Personnel Cannot Be Determined

As part of the core contract personnel inventory, IC CHCO collects information from the elements on contractor-performed functions using the primary contractor occupation and competency expertise data field. An IC CHCO official explained that this data field should reflect the tasks performed by the contract personnel. IC CHCO's guidance for this data field instructs the IC elements to select one option from a list of over 20 broad categories of functions for each contract entry in the inventory. Based on our review of relevant contract documents, such as statements of work, we were able to verify the primary contractor occupation and competency expertise reported for almost all of the records we reviewed. Using the primary contractor occupation and competency expertise data field in the core contract personnel inventory, the civilian IC elements reported functions performed such as human capital, information technology, program management, administration, collection and operations, and security services, among others.

While we could verify the categories of functions performed for the contracts we reviewed, we could not determine the extent to which civilian IC elements contracted for these functions. Limitations we identified in the obligation and FTE data reported in the inventory precluded us from using the information on contractor functions to determine the number of personnel and their costs associated with each function category. For example, we were able to verify for one State INR contract that contract personnel performed functions within the systems engineering category, but we could not determine the number of personnel dedicated to that function because of unreliable obligation and FTE data.

In addition, IC CHCO provides information on contractor functions in its reports and briefings to Congress. However, it does not include the information it collects through the inventory's primary contractor occupation and competency expertise data field. IC CHCO instead uses the budget category data field in the inventory as its source for information on functions performed by core contractor personnel, citing a desire for information provided to Congress to align with the budget request. The budget category data field, however, reflects a contract's funding source rather than the functions performed by personnel working under these contracts. By using budget category information as a proxy for contractor functions, IC CHCO does not adhere to leading practices outlined in OMB guidelines for disseminated information.[29] OMB guidelines provide that agencies should ensure that disseminated information be accurate, clear, and useful to the intended users. IC CHCO and civilian IC element officials acknowledged that the budget category is not the best representation of the functions performed by contractors. For example, we found contracts from one civilian IC element that were reported as collection and operations for the budget category, as required by IC CHCO guidance, included services such as policy and program development support, information technology, and administration.[30]

Data on Reasons for Contractor Use Not Supported by Documentation and Do Not Always Provide Insight

The reasons that the civilian IC elements use core contract personnel could not be reliably determined from the core contract personnel inventory information due to a lack of documentation to corroborate the reasons reported in the inventory. In preparing their inventory submissions, IC elements can select one of eight response options for the reason data field (see table 1).

However, we could not verify the information reported by the civilian IC elements in the inventory due to a lack of corroborating documentation. For the 81 of the 102 records in our sample coded as unique expertise, we did not find evidence in the statements of work or other contract documents that the functions performed by the contractors required expertise not otherwise available from U.S. government civilian or military personnel. For example, ODNI contracts coded as unique expertise included services for conducting workshops and analysis, producing financial statements, and providing program management. Based on inventory submissions by both the civilian and military IC elements, IC CHCO reported to Congress that for fiscal year 2011, 57 percent of the core contract personnel FTEs were contracted for their unique expertise.

Further, we found that the most widely used reason response option among the records we reviewed—specified service—does not provide insight into the civilian IC elements' reasons for using core contract personnel. Instead, this response option describes the nature of the contract. Of the 287 records we reviewed, civilian IC elements selected specified service as the reason for the contract for 45 percent of those records. For example, an official from one civilian IC element stated that they selected specified service for all of their contracts in the fiscal years 2010 and 2011 inventories because, in accordance with the definition, they were buying services. However, these officials also cited the need for contractors due to personnel restrictions and budgetary considerations, which could correspond to the insufficient staffing resources response option.

Civilian IC element officials noted that the reasons for contractor use reported in the inventory are subjective and based on the knowledge of the contracting or program official at the time of reporting. IC CHCO does not require elements to maintain supporting documentation for their contract reason codes. As a result, the civilian IC elements could not provide documentation for 40 percent of the records we reviewed. Additionally, an official from one civilian IC element told us that there was confusion among program offices responsible for determining the reason code as to the specific meaning of certain response options for the reason code. Civilian IC element officials stated that multiple reasons could pertain for utilizing the contract, but they can only select one option for the purposes of the inventory. For example, while officials from one civilian IC element stated that many of their contractors are brought on board for their institutional knowledge and skills, this element's inventory data does not reflect the transfer of institutional knowledge reason code for any of their reported contracts. Most of this element's contracts were coded as unique expertise, more efficient or effective, and specified service, which were supported by the contract documents. Due to the subjectivity of the coding, combined with the capability to only select one response and without requiring supporting documentation, the reasons identified in the civilian IC elements' inventory submissions do not fully reflect why they use core contract personnel.

Table 1. Available Response Options in the Core Contract Personnel Inventory for IC Elements to Report on Reasons for Using Contractors

Reason for using contract personnel	Definition of reason from IC CHCO guidance
Discrete non-recurring task	To accomplish a discrete, nonrecurring, or temporary project, work assignment, or task of definite duration or deliverable, such that the contract ends when the project, assignment, or task is completed.

Table 1. (Continued)

Reason for using contract personnel	Definition of reason from IC CHCO guidance
Immediate surge	To provide surge support for a particular IC mission area. In this regard, the use of a contractor enables the IC element to rapidly expand to meet a mission or business exigency, and then curtail that contract support when the exigency passes. A surge requirement may be of extended duration.
Insufficient staffing resources	To perform work that would otherwise have been provided by a U.S. Government civilian given sufficient resources.
More efficient or effective	To provide support or administrative services, where the provision of such services by contract personnel is determined to be effective or efficient.
Specified service	To provide a specified service, including technical assistance, in support of a core mission or function, where that service is of indefinite quantity.
Transfer of institutional knowledge	To maintain critical continuity or skills in support of a particular mission or functional area in the face of skills gaps, the loss (anticipated or otherwise) of mission-essential U.S. Government civilian or military personnel, or other similar exigency.
Unique expertise	To provide unique technical, professional, managerial, or intellectual expertise to the IC element, where such expertise is not otherwise available from U.S. Governmental civilian or military personnel.
Other	Requires explanation in contractor inventory comments.

Source: IC CHCO.

LIMITED PROGRESS HAS BEEN MADE IN DEVELOPING POLICIES AND STRATEGIES ON CONTRACTOR USE TO MITIGATE RISKS

CIA, ODNI, and the executive departments, which are responsible for developing policies to address risks related to contractors for the other six civilian IC elements within those departments, have generally made limited progress in developing such policies. Further, the eight civilian IC elements have generally not developed strategic workforce plans that address contractor use. While DHS and State have issued policies and guidance that address generally all of OFPP Policy Letter 11-01's requirements related to contracting for services that closely support inherently governmental functions, the other departments, CIA, and ODNI are in various stages of developing required internal policies to address the policy letter. In addition, the civilian IC elements' decisions to use contractors are generally not informed by strategic workforce plans or other strategic-level guidance on the appropriate mix of government and contract personnel for functions that are critical to elements' missions. The civilian IC elements' ability to use the core contract personnel inventory as a strategic workforce planning tool is hindered because the inventory does not provide these elements insight into the functions performed by contractors or the extent to which contractors are performing functions that closely support inherently governmental functions or are critical. Without guidance, strategies, and tools related to services that closely support inherently governmental functions and critical functions, the civilian IC elements may not be well-positioned to identify and manage the related risks of contracting for those functions.

CIA, ODNI, and Departments of the Other Civilian IC Elements Have Not Fully Developed Policies That Address Risks Associated with Contractors Supporting Inherently Governmental Functions

OFPP Policy Letter 11-01's requirements related to contracting for services that closely support inherently governmental functions include giving special consideration to using federal employees to perform these functions, and if contractors are used to perform such work, giving special management attention to contractors' activities. The policy letter includes a checklist of responsibilities that must be carried out when agencies rely on contractors to perform these functions and requires agencies to develop and maintain internal procedures to address the requirements of the guidance. OFPP, however, did not establish a deadline for when agencies need to complete these procedures. In 2011, we concluded that a deadline may help better focus agency efforts to address risks and therefore recommended that OFPP establish a near-term deadline for agencies to develop internal procedures, including for services that closely support inherently governmental functions. OFPP generally concurred with our recommendation and commented that it would likely establish time frames for agencies to develop the required internal procedures, but it has not yet done so.[31]

We assessed the extent to which CIA, ODNI, and the executive departments of the other civilian IC elements—DHS, DOE, DOJ, State, and Treasury—developed internal procedures to address the policy letter because the civilian IC elements within departments are not required to develop their own procedures to address the policy letter. The departmental civilian IC elements are subject to policies and guidance at the department level for considering and managing risks related to contracting for services that closely support inherently governmental functions. Our analysis found that DHS and State have issued policies and guidance that generally address all of these requirements, but CIA, ODNI, and the other three departments have not fully developed policies to do so.

Civilian IC element and department officials cited various reasons for not yet developing policies to address all of the OFPP policy letter's requirements. For example, Treasury officials stated that the OFPP policy letter called for dramatic changes in agency procedures and thus elected to conduct a number of pilots before making policy changes. DOE officials stated that they are waiting for revisions to the Federal Acquisition Regulation, which would incorporate the OFPP policy letter's requirements, before reviewing and updating their acquisition policies as necessary.

Decisions to Use Contractors Not Guided by Strategies on Appropriate Mix of Government and Contract Personnel

OMB's July 2009 memorandum on managing the multisector workforce and our prior work on best practices in strategic human capital management have indicated that agencies' strategic workforce plans should address the extent to which it is appropriate to use contractors.[32] The civilian IC elements' current strategic workforce plans, however, generally do not address the extent to which it is appropriate to use contractors, either in general or more specifically to perform critical functions, as called for in the OMB guidance. For example, ODNI's 2012-2017 strategic human capital plan outlines the current mix of government and contract personnel by five broad function types: core mission, enablers, leadership, oversight, and other. The plan, however, does not elaborate on what the appropriate mix of government and contract personnel should be on a function-by-function basis. The plan also discusses efforts to reduce the number of core contract personnel but does not elaborate on particular functions to target. In August 2013, ODNI officials informed us they are continuing to develop documentation to address a workforce plan.

Civilian IC element officials stated that their decisions to use contractors are made on a case-by-case basis and that budgetary considerations, government personnel ceilings, and the cost-effectiveness of contractors are key factors in their decisions on whether to use contractors. For example, officials from several civilian IC elements stated that due to recent budgetary considerations, they have made efforts to reduce their reliance on contractors, in part by converting contractor positions to government positions when possible. OMB's July 2009 memorandum on managing the multisector workforce, however, indicates that assessments of the appropriate workforce mix should generally not focus around a particular outcome, such as reducing the number of contractors.[33] The memorandum indicates that agencies should identify which types of work should be done by government personnel and contract personnel based on program goals, priorities, and associated human capital needs.

While IC CHCO requires IC elements to conduct strategic workforce planning and prepare a human capital employment plan, neither effort requires the elements to determine the appropriate mix of personnel either generally or on a function-by-function basis. ICD 612 directs IC elements to determine, review, and evaluate the number and uses of core contract personnel when conducting strategic workforce planning but does not reference the requirements related to determining the appropriate workforce mix specified in OMB's July 2009 memorandum or require elements to document the extent to which contractors should be used. IC CHCO also required IC elements to submit a 2012-2016 human capital employment plan, which was to include information on the current workforce mix and expected changes as well as information on elements' efforts to examine the mix of government and contract personnel, as appropriate. One IC CHCO official, however, explained that some IC elements' strategic workforce planning efforts are more robust than others, so the level of detail and information provided in the plans vary widely across the IC elements. Nevertheless, irrespective of an agency's size, OMB's guidance on managing the multisector workforce notes that agencies that have a strategic understanding of their current and appropriate mix of personnel for each function are better positioned to build and sustain the internal capacity necessary to maintain control over their missions and operations.

Civilian IC Elements' Ability to Use Inventory for Strategic Planning Hindered by Limited Information on Contractor Functions

OFPP's November 2010 memorandum on service contract inventories indicates that a service contract inventory is a tool that can assist an agency in conducting strategic workforce planning.[34] Specifically, an agency can gain insight into the extent to which contractors are being used to perform specific services by analyzing how contracted resources, such as contract obligations and FTEs, are distributed by function across an agency. The memorandum further indicates that this insight is especially important for contracts whose performance may involve critical functions or functions closely associated with inherently governmental functions. OFPP officials stated that the IC's core contract personnel inventory serves this purpose for the IC and, to some extent, follows the intent of the service contract inventories guidance to help mitigate risks. OFPP officials stated that IC elements are not required to submit separate service contract inventories that are required of the civilian agencies and DOD, in part because of the classified nature of some of the contracts. The core contract personnel inventory, however, does not provide the civilian IC elements with detailed insight into the functions their contractors are performing or the extent to which contractors are used to perform functions that support their missions and closely support inherently governmental work. Without complete and accurate information in the core contract personnel inventory on the extent to which contractors are performing specific functions, the civilian IC elements may be missing an opportunity to leverage the inventory as a tool for conducting strategic workforce planning and for prioritizing contracts that may require increased management attention and oversight.

We found that the data reported by the civilian IC elements in the primary contractor occupation and competency expertise data field accurately reflect the broad categories of contracted functions for each contract, but these data do not provide detailed information on the functions performed by contractors. Based on the contract documents we reviewed, such as statements of work, we identified at least 128 instances in the 287 records we reviewed in which the primary contractor occupation and competency expertise data field did not reflect the full range of services listed in the contracts. This was due in part to IC CHCO's guidance, which instructs the elements to select only one service from the list of multiple response options for each contract entry in the inventory. An IC CHCO official explained that elements are instructed to select the predominant type of service provided by the contract given that elements are not able to record more than one type of service purchased for each contract. The civilian IC element officials acknowledged that the primary contractor occupation and competency expertise coding is not fully reflective of the services the contractors are performing.

IC CHCO's guidance, including ICD 612 and core contract personnel inventory guidance, do not require the elements to review all of their contracts, including classified contracts, to ensure that they identify and manage risks related to contracts for services that closely support inherently governmental or critical functions. In contrast, the civilian executive agencies are statutorily required to compile an annual service contract inventory, and as part of the inventory review process, agencies are required to ensure that they are not using contract personnel to perform critical functions in such a way that could affect the ability of the agency to maintain control of its mission and operations and giving special management attention to functions that closely support inherently governmental functions. However, certain civilian IC elements' contracts, along with classified contracts at the civilian IC elements, are excluded from the civilian agencies' service contract inventories. For those elements with contracts that are excluded from the civilian agencies' service contract inventories, identifying which contracts contain these types of functions in the core contract personnel inventory could help target agencies' efforts to provide enhanced management attention.

CONCLUSION

The eight civilian IC elements, like other federal agencies, have long relied on contractors to support their missions. In fiscal year 2006, IC CHCO initiated data collection efforts for the core contract personnel inventory to collect information from elements on their use of these personnel and to report to Congress on the number of core contract personnel and their associated costs. IC CHCO and the civilian IC elements have taken and continue to take steps to improve the reliability of the reported information, such as standardizing how FTEs will be calculated for the fiscal year 2012 inventory. These are positive steps. Nevertheless, we identified several limitations, including definitional changes, inaccurate data, methodological differences, and poor documentation, that collectively undermine the utility of the information for determining the extent to which the civilian IC elements rely on core contract personnel. As a result, the IC CHCO cannot reliably report on statutorily required information comparing the number and cost of core contract personnel over time. By enhancing their internal controls, the civilian IC elements can help ensure that the data being reported to Congress are as accurate and complete as possible and consistent with OMB guidelines. Further, inherent limitations or changes in definitions or methodologies, including those intended to improve the data, can affect data accuracy, completeness, and comparability. Not fully disclosing these limitations and the effects of these changes limits the transparency and usefulness of the information reported to Congress.

Within the IC, core contract personnel perform functions that could influence the direction and control of key aspects of the U.S. intelligence mission, such as intelligence analysis and operations. Our prior work and OMB policies have underscored the importance of agencies having guidance, strategies, and reliable data to inform decisions related to the appropriate use of contractor personnel. Building on longstanding OMB policy, OFPP's September 2011 guidance requires agencies to develop internal procedures to identify and oversee contractors providing services that closely support inherently governmental functions. Yet, of the agencies we reviewed, ODNI, CIA, DOJ, DOE, and Treasury have not fully developed such procedures or established required time frames for doing so. Without these procedures in place, ODNI, CIA, and the civilian IC elements within these three departments risk not taking appropriate steps to manage and oversee contract personnel, particularly those performing work that could influence government decision making. In an effort to help manage the use of contractor personnel within the IC, elements are required by ICD 612 to conduct strategic workforce planning related to their use of core contract personnel. However, ICD 612 falls short of OMB's July 2009 memorandum on managing the multisector workforce by not requiring the elements to document their assessment of the appropriate use of contractors or the appropriate mix of government and contractor personnel on a function-by-function basis. One tool identified by OFPP that can help agencies plan for the use of contract personnel and mitigate associated risks is a service contract inventory, which for the IC is the annual core contract personnel inventory. Yet, as it is currently structured, the core contract personnel inventory is limited in its ability to be an effective tool for doing so. As a result, the civilian IC elements cannot use the inventory to identify those services that require increased management attention under OFPP's September 2011 guidance. Additionally, ICD 612 and other IC CHCO guidance do not require elements to identify in the inventory those contracts that provide critical services or those that closely support inherently governmental functions. Consequently, civilian IC elements or their respective departments we reviewed are not well-positioned to assess the potential effects of relying on contractor personnel who perform such functions.

RECOMMENDATIONS FOR EXECUTIVE ACTION

To improve congressional oversight and enhance civilian IC elements' insights into their use of core contract personnel, we recommend that IC CHCO take the following two actions:

- When reporting to congressional committees, clearly specify limitations and significant methodological changes and their associated effects and
- In coordination with the IC elements, develop a plan to enhance internal controls for compiling the annual core contract personnel inventory. Such a plan could include requiring IC elements to document their methodologies for determining the number and costs of core contract personnel and the steps the elements took for ensuring data accuracy and completeness.

To improve civilian IC elements' or their respective departments' ability to mitigate risks associated with the use of contractors, we recommend the Director of National Intelligence, Director of the Central Intelligence Agency, Attorney General of the United States, and Secretaries of Energy and the Treasury direct responsible agency officials to set time frames to develop guidance that fully addresses OFPP Policy Letter 11-01's requirements related to closely supporting inherently governmental functions.

To improve the ability of the civilian IC elements to strategically plan for their contractors and mitigate associated risks, we recommend that IC CHCO take the following three actions:

- Revise ICD 612's provisions governing strategic workforce planning to require the IC elements to identify their assessment of the appropriate workforce mix on a function-by-function basis;
- Assess options for how the core contract personnel inventory could be modified to provide better insights into the functions performed by contractors when there are multiple services provided under a contract; and

- Require the IC elements to identify contracts within the core contract personnel inventory that include services that are critical or closely support inherently governmental functions.

AGENCY COMMENTS AND OUR EVALUATION

We provided a draft of our September 2013 classified report to CIA, DHS, DOE, DOJ, ODNI, State, and Treasury for review and comment. We received written comments from ODNI, as well as technical comments that we incorporated into the draft as appropriate. In its written comments, ODNI generally agreed with the six recommendations that we directed to it.

With regard to our first recommendation to clearly specify limitations and significant methodological changes and their associated effects when reporting on the IC's use of core contract personnel, ODNI agreed that IC CHCO will highlight all adjustments to the data over time and the implications of those adjustments in future briefings to Congress and OMB. Similarly, ODNI agreed with our second recommendation to develop a plan to enhance internal controls for compiling the annual core contract personnel inventory. ODNI stated that IC CHCO, in coordination with the IC Chief Financial Office, has added requirements for the IC elements to include the methodologies used to identify and count the number of core contract personnel and their steps for ensuring the accuracy and completeness of the data. ODNI further stated that IC CHCO intends to request the methodologies used by the IC elements for the fiscal year 2014 budget data call, which includes the core contract personnel inventory.

In commenting on our third recommendation, ODNI proposed that when ICD 612 is revised, IC CHCO will request notification on the mechanism by which each IC element adheres to OFPP Policy Letter 11-01. We believe IC CHCO's proposal to monitor the IC elements' implementation of OFPP Policy Letter 11-01 can help improve policies and guidance to mitigate the risks associated with using contractors across the IC. ODNI, however, did not directly address whether it will set time frames to develop guidance for use within ODNI to fully address OFPP Policy Letter 11-01's requirements. We continue to believe that ODNI as an IC element should set timeframes to develop its own guidance that fully addresses the OFPP policy letter.

With regard to our fourth recommendation to revise ICD 612's provisions governing strategic workforce planning, ODNI stated that IC CHCO has recognized the need to update ICD 612 and will work to determine the most appropriate mechanism to identify the functions performed within a contract. ODNI further noted that IC CHCO proposed that IC elements be responsible for ensuring they are addressing the appropriate workforce mix when conducting workforce planning rather than requiring this information as part of core contract personnel inventory data collection efforts. We believe that ODNI's comments are consistent with our recommendation.

Regarding our fifth recommendation to assess options for how the core contract personnel inventory could be modified to provide better insights into the functions performed by contractors when multiple services are provided under a contract, ODNI stated that IC CHCO will examine the requirement to provide insights into all functions under a contract to determine if there is a need to modify the inventory to capture that level of information. As we note in our report, having better insight into contractor functions through the core contract personnel inventory can help the civilian IC elements conduct strategic workforce planning and prioritize contracts that may require increased management attention and oversight.

For our sixth recommendation to require the IC elements to identify contracts within the core contract personnel inventory that include critical services or those closely supporting inherently governmental functions, ODNI stated it will explore doing so. ODNI noted in its comments that the definition of core contract personnel in ICD 612 is already aligned with OFFP Policy Letter 11-01's definition of contract personnel who perform services that closely support inherently governmental functions. As we note in our report, however, not all core contract personnel perform functions that closely support inherently governmental functions and therefore do not need enhanced management oversight required by OFPP. Further, the definition of core contract personnel does not identify those functions that are critical to an agency's mission. OFPP Policy Letter 11-01 requires agencies to take different steps to manage the risks related to contractors performing critical functions, such as ensuring government personnel perform or manage these functions to the extent necessary to maintain control of their missions and operations. Clearly identifying which contracts within the core contract personnel inventory include services that closely support inherently governmental functions as well as those that include critical functions will better position the civilian IC elements to assess the potential effects of relying on contract personnel who perform such functions and take any necessary actions to mitigate risks.

CIA, DOE, DOJ, and Treasury did not comment on our recommendation to them but generally provided technical comments that we incorporated into the draft as appropriate. DHS and State also provided technical comments which we incorporated as appropriate.

Timothy J. DiNapoli
Director
Acquisition and Sourcing Management

APPENDIX I. OBJECTIVES, SCOPE, AND METHODOLOGY

The objectives of this review were to determine (1) the extent to which the civilian intelligence community (IC) elements rely on core contract personnel; (2) the functions performed by core contract personnel and the factors that contribute to their use; and (3) whether the civilian IC elements have developed policies and guidance and strategically planned for their use of these contract personnel to mitigate related risks. The eight civilian IC elements covered by our review are the Central Intelligence Agency (CIA), the Department of Energy's Office of Intelligence and Counterintelligence (DOE IN), Department of Homeland Security's Office of Intelligence and Analysis (DHS I&A), Department of State's Bureau of Intelligence and Research (State INR), Department of the Treasury's Office of Intelligence and Analysis (Treasury OIA), Drug Enforcement Administration's Office of National Security Intelligence (DEA NN), Federal Bureau of Investigation (FBI), and Office of the Director of National Intelligence (ODNI).[35]

To address our first and second objectives, we examined the civilian IC elements' submissions to the fiscal years 2007 to 2011 core contract personnel inventories, when available. The submissions contain information on the elements' core contracts from over 10 data fields, which vary by fiscal year. For the purposes of answering the first and second objectives, we focused on five data fields related to the elements' extent of reliance on core contract personnel, the functions performed by these contract personnel, and the factors that contributed to their use: fiscal year obligations, total full-time equivalents (FTE), primary contractor occupation and competency expertise, budget category, and reason code. We were not able to assess the reliability of the information reported for these data fields in the elements' submissions to the fiscal years 2007 to 2009 inventories for various reasons, such as elements not having records of their submissions for certain years. In addition, the information reported for the fiscal year obligations, total FTEs, budget category, and reason code data fields in the elements' submissions to the fiscal years 2010 to 2011 inventories was not sufficiently reliable for our intended purposes of determining the civilian IC elements' extent of reliance on core contract personnel, the functions performed by these personnel, or the factors that contribute to their use. We present this information with the associated limitations in the report where appropriate. Although we identified some limitations, the primary contractor occupation and competency expertise data field was sufficiently reliable for identifying the general types of functions performed. However, because neither the fiscal year obligations nor total FTEs data field was sufficiently reliable, we could not determine the extent to which the civilian IC elements use contract personnel to perform certain functions based on the primary contractor occupation and competency expertise data field. Appendix II contains a more detailed discussion of our sampling methodology and data reliability assessment.

We also reviewed the Intelligence Community Chief Human Capital Officer's (IC CHCO) annual guidance to elements for preparing their submissions to the fiscal years 2007 to 2012 inventories and information reported in annual core contract personnel inventory briefings and personnel level assessments provided to Congress. We interviewed officials at IC CHCO and the eight civilian IC elements on the processes for collecting and reporting their information for the inventory.

To address our third objective, we compared the civilian IC elements' or their respective departments' relevant guidance, planning documents, and tools related to their use of contractors to Office of Management and Budget (OMB) guidance that address risks related to relying on contractors. We reviewed Office of Federal Procurement Policy (OFPP) Policy Letter 11-01 and compared the policy letter's requirements addressing contracting for closely supporting inherently governmental functions to civilian IC elements' or their respective departments' acquisition policies and guidance to determine the extent to which the requirements were met.[36] We reviewed OMB's July 2009 Memorandum on Managing the Multisector Workforce and GAO's prior work on strategic human capital best practices and compared the leading practices identified to the strategic workforce planning requirement in Intelligence Community Directive (ICD) 612 and civilian IC elements' strategic human capital or other workforce plans to determine the extent to which the leading practices were implemented.[37] We reviewed the leading practices identified in OMB's November 2010 and December 2011 memoranda on service contract inventories and the civilian IC elements' data on functions performed by contractors.[38] We reviewed IC CHCO guidance on core contract personnel to determine the extent to which it addressed services that closely support inherently governmental functions and critical functions. We also interviewed human capital, procurement, or program officials at each civilian IC element to discuss ongoing efforts related to strategic planning and developing policies to mitigate risks from each IC element or their respective departments.

ODNI, in consultation with the other civilian IC elements, deemed some of the information in the September 2013 report as classified, which must be protected from public disclosure. Therefore, this report omits sensitive information about (1) the number and associated costs of government and core contract personnel and some details on how the civilian IC elements prepare the core contract personnel inventory, (2) specific contracts from civilian IC elements we reviewed, and (3) details related to the civilian IC elements' or their respective departments' progress in developing policies to mitigate risks related to contractors and the civilian IC elements' strategic workforce planning efforts.

We conducted this performance audit from November 2012 to September 2013 in accordance with generally accepted government auditing standards. We subsequently worked with ODNI from September 2013 to December 2013 to prepare an unclassified version of this report for public release. Government auditing standards require that we plan and perform the audit to obtain sufficient, appropriate evidence to provide a reasonable basis for our findings and conclusions based on our audit objectives. We believe that the evidence obtained provides a reasonable basis for our findings and conclusions based on our audit objectives.

APPENDIX II. OBSERVATIONS ON RELIABILITY OF EIGHT CIVILIAN INTELLIGENCE COMMUNITY ELEMENTS' INVENTORY DATA SUBMISSIONS

We conducted an analysis to determine whether the eight civilian intelligence community (IC) elements' submissions to the fiscal years 2007 to 2011 core contract personnel inventories were sufficiently reliable for the purpose of identifying the extent to which these elements have relied on core contract personnel, the functions performed by these contract personnel, and the factors that contributed to their use.[39] We examined data fields from the submissions related to these purposes, including the amount of obligations (fiscal year obligations), the number of contractor full-time equivalents (total FTEs), the types of functions performed by the contract personnel (primary contractor occupation and competency expertise), the type of funding used for the contract (budget category), and the reason for using contract personnel to perform a service (reason code).[40] In addition, we reviewed the Intelligence Community Chief Human Capital Officer's (IC CHCO) guidance to the elements for preparing their submissions and interviewed civilian IC element officials on their processes for compiling and reporting the information. We could not determine the reliability of the information reported for these data fields in the elements' submissions to the fiscal years 2007 to 2009 inventories. In addition, we identified several concerns with the reliability of the information reported for the fiscal year obligations, total FTEs, budget category, and reason code data fields in the civilian IC elements' submissions to the fiscal years 2010 and 2011 inventories. As a result, we determined that the data in these submissions were not sufficiently reliable for the purposes of our review.[41] Although we identified some limitations, the primary contractor occupation and competency expertise data field was sufficiently reliable for identifying the broad types of functions performed. However, because neither the fiscal year obligations nor total FTEs data fields was sufficiently reliable, we could not determine the extent to which the civilian IC elements use contract personnel to perform certain functions based on the primary contractor occupation and competency expertise data field.

Methodology

To determine the extent to which the civilian IC elements relied on core contract personnel, the functions performed by these contract personnel, and the factors that contributed to their use, we examined data from the eight civilian IC elements' submissions to the core contract personnel inventory: fiscal year obligations, total FTEs, budget category, reason code, and primary contractor occupation and competency expertise. We planned to examine these five data fields for the civilian IC elements' submissions to the fiscal years 2007 to 2011 inventories. We chose to assess the submissions for fiscal years 2007 to 2011 because IC CHCO published the first inventory in fiscal year 2007, and the fiscal year 2011 inventory was the most recent data available at the time we started our review.[42] In addition, we chose to analyze data for these five fields because they were related to our audit objectives.

We planned to review the civilian IC elements' submissions to the fiscal years 2007 to 2011 core contract personnel inventories. However, we could not determine the reliability of their submissions for the fiscal years 2007 to

2009 inventories for various reasons. For all but one of these elements, we were unable to assess at least one year of data because (1) element officials told us they did not have records of the data they submitted to IC CHCO, (2) element officials told us they had specific concerns about the reliability of data reported in certain fiscal years that would make it difficult for us to verify the data, or (3) obtaining relevant documentation would require an unreasonable amount of time. As a result, we assessed the reliability of the five data fields from the elements' submissions to the fiscal years 2010 and 2011 inventories because we could assess the data for at least a majority of the elements for these years.

To determine whether the five data fields from the civilian IC elements' submissions to the fiscal years 2010 and 2011 inventories would be reliable for the purpose of our review, we interviewed IC CHCO and civilian IC element officials knowledgeable about the processes for compiling and reporting the information. In addition, we reviewed IC CHCO's guidance to elements for preparing their submissions. We also assessed the accuracy, consistency, and completeness of the data in the submissions by analyzing the five data fields from the civilian IC elements' submissions. We compared the information reported to information in relevant documentation for a sample of 287 records— representing 222 contracts or purchase orders.[43] For elements that reported 30 or fewer records in either fiscal year, we reviewed data for all reported records for both fiscal years. For elements that reported more than 30 records in either fiscal year, we selected a random, nongeneralizable sample of records from their submissions.[44]

We reviewed relevant documents to determine whether they validated the information reported in the civilian IC elements' submissions to the fiscal year 2010 and 2011 core contract personnel inventories for the five data fields for each record in the sample. Table 2 below summarizes our criteria for making these determinations for each data field.

After our initial review of the documents, we provided the civilian IC elements with an overview of our determinations that indicated whether the documentation validated the information reported. In addition, we offered these elements an opportunity to provide additional documentation for records in which we identified discrepancies with the documents or lacked sufficient information to validate the reported data. In the instances in which elements provided additional documentation, we reviewed the documents and made adjustments to our determinations, as appropriate.

Results of Analysis

We made the following determinations of whether the information reported for the five data fields was sufficiently reliable for our intended purposes.

Fiscal Year Obligations

We determined that the information reported for the fiscal year obligations data field was not sufficiently reliable for our intended purpose of identifying the eight civilian IC elements' extent of reliance on core contract personnel for several reasons. First, we could only validate the amount of obligations reported for approximately 62 percent of the records we reviewed. For an additional 21 percent of the records we reviewed, the civilian IC elements either under- or over-reported the amount of obligations by more than 10 percent.

Second, we identified inconsistencies between civilian IC elements' methodologies for reporting the amount of obligations. Officials from six of the civilian IC elements stated that they reported the amount of obligations on core contracts that are active at any point within a given fiscal year while officials from two of the civilian IC elements told us they do not report the amount of obligations on certain contracts if they are not active on the date of reporting. As a result, the information reported cannot be compared across the eight civilian IC elements.

Table 2. Criteria for Determining Whether Relevant Documents Validated Information Reported in Eight Civilian IC Elements' Submissions to the Fiscal Years 2010 and 2011 Core Contract Personnel Inventories

Data field	Criteria for determining whether documents validated information reported
Fiscal year obligations	We reviewed documents, such as the contract award or modifications signed in a given fiscal year, to determine the amount of funds obligated within a given fiscal year. If the total obligations identified were within 10 percent of the amount of obligations reported for the respective record in the submission, we considered the amount reported to be validated by available documents.

Table 2. (Continued)

Data field	Criteria for determining whether documents validated information reported
Total FTEs	We reviewed documents, such as contractor invoices or contract award documents, to determine the number of FTEs for each record. For those records with at least 10 FTEs, if the number of FTEs we calculated was within 10 percent of the number of FTEs reported, then we considered the number reported to be supported by available documents. For those records with fewer than 10 FTEs, if the number of FTEs we calculated was within 1 FTE, then we considered the number reported to be validated.
Budget category	Only CIA and ODNI provided documents that would allow us to validate this data field.[a] We reviewed the budget line item to determine whether the budget category reported for each record was accurate.
Reason code	We reviewed documents, such as the statement of work or justification for other than full and open competition, to determine whether the selected reason code category for each record was validated.
Primary contractor occupation and competency expertise	We reviewed documents such as the statement of work to identify the types of functions performed by the contract personnel and determined whether the selected category reflected the information in the documents.

Source: GAO.

[a] The other civilian IC elements did not provide sufficient documentation for us to validate the information reported for the records we reviewed.

Lastly, the amount of obligations reported for two of the civilian IC elements does not reflect all of the obligations in a given fiscal year. First, these elements' methodology would exclude certain obligations on core contracts that are active at some point during a fiscal year but not on the date of reporting. We were unable to determine the magnitude of obligations not included in the inventory because we did not have a way to identify contracts not reported by the civilian IC elements. Further, officials from these two elements stated that they also do not report obligations on contract option periods that are no longer active on the date of reporting even if the contract is active at that time.

Total FTEs

We determined that the information reported for the total FTEs data field was not sufficiently reliable for our intended purpose of identifying the eight civilian IC elements' extent of reliance on core contract personnel. First, the elements could not provide complete or readily available documentation to validate the information reported for approximately 37 percent of the records.[45]

Second, we identified inconsistencies in civilian IC elements' methodologies for calculating the number of FTEs in their submissions to the fiscal years 2010 and 2011 inventories, thus limiting our ability to compare the number of FTEs reported across the elements. The civilian IC elements reported the number of FTEs by: (1) calculating estimates based on target labor hours, (2) calculating the number of labor hours invoiced by the contractor, (3) counting the number of contract personnel on board on a selected date and the number of approved contractor vacancies, or (4) using the amount of obligations and average labor hour rates.

Lastly, as noted above, officials from two of the civilian IC elements stated that they do not report certain contracts in their submissions if they are not active on the date of reporting.

As a result, the number of FTEs on core contracts that are active at some point during a fiscal year but not on the date of reporting would not be reflected in these two elements' submissions. We were unable to determine the magnitude of the number of FTEs not included in the inventory because we did not have a way to identify contracts not reported by these two elements.

Budget Category

We determined that the information reported for the budget category data field in the eight civilian IC elements' submissions was not sufficiently reliable for our intended purpose of identifying the types of functions performed by core contract personnel. We intended to use this data field to describe the types of functions performed by core contract personnel because IC CHCO uses the budget category in its briefings to Congress to provide information on the functions performed by core contract personnel. The IC CHCO core contract personnel inventory guidance instructs the elements to complete the budget category data field by reporting where the funding for the contract is assigned according to the Congressional Budget Justification Books. Civilian IC element officials acknowledged that the budget category is not the best representation of the functions being performed by contractors. Based on our review of documents, we found that contracted functions are not necessarily reflected by the budget category designation. Further, we identified discrepancies between the budget category information reported and the information contained in relevant documents for approximately one-third of the records we reviewed for two of the civilian IC elements. Based on our review of the documents provided, the reported budget category information for one of these elements improved from fiscal year 2010 to 2011. However, we still identified discrepancies between the information reported and relevant documents for 23 percent of the records we reviewed.

Reason Code

We determined that the information reported for the reason code data field in the eight civilian IC elements' submissions was not sufficiently reliable for our intended purpose of identifying the factors for using core contract personnel because we could not determine the reliability of the information reported for a significant number of the records we reviewed. We could not validate the reported reason code based on the information in the documents provided for approximately 40 percent of the records we reviewed. Further, this percentage is even more pronounced for those records coded as a category other than specified service, which is a broad category defined as when the service being provided is of indefinite quantity. The civilian IC elements selected specified service for approximately 45 percent of the records we reviewed. For the 156 remaining records coded as a category other than specified service, we could not validate the information reported for approximately 73 percent of the records.

In addition, we identified instances when multiple selection options could apply to a record. IC CHCO guidance requires elements to select one category per record. However, civilian IC element officials acknowledged that more than one response option can apply to a record and that officials at the time of reporting make a subjective determination of which option best applies. As a result, the subjective nature of the determination and that more than one record could apply to a record raises concerns about the consistency of the information reported.

Lastly, because we determined that the fiscal year obligations and total FTEs data fields were not sufficiently reliable for determining the extent of reliance on core contract personnel, we would not be able to use the information reported for these data fields to describe the extent to which the civilian IC elements used these personnel for particular reasons based on the reason code data field.

Primary Contractor Occupation and Competency Expertise

Although we identified some limitations, the information reported for the primary contractor occupation and competency expertise data field is sufficiently reliable for our intended purpose of identifying the types of functions performed by core contract personnel. Based on our review of relevant documents, we were able to find support for the selected response option for almost all of the records we reviewed.

However, we identified some limitations that would limit insight into the functions performed by the contract personnel. First, we identified instances when multiple selection options could apply to a record. The core contract personnel inventory guidance instructs the elements to select only one response option for each record.

Based on the documents provided, we identified at least 128 instances in the 287 records we reviewed in which the primary contractor occupation and competency expertise data field did not reflect the full range of services listed in the documents.

Civilian IC element officials acknowledged that the primary contractor occupation and competency expertise coding are not fully reflective of the services the contractors are performing.

As a result, the information may not be consistently reported given the subjective nature of this data field.

Further, we identified a limited number of instances when the information may not be consistently reported as a function performed by the contract personnel.

For example, an element may make a selection based on the mission the contractor supported or the contractor's general area of expertise rather than the type of function performed.

Lastly, because we determined that the fiscal year obligations and total FTEs data fields were not sufficiently reliable for determining the extent of reliance on core contract personnel, we would not be able to use the information reported for these data fields to describe the extent to which the contract personnel performed certain types of functions based on the primary contractor occupation and competency expertise data field.

APPENDIX III. OVERVIEW OF THE EIGHT CIVILIAN INTELLIGENCE COMMUNITY ELEMENTS AND THEIR RESPECTIVE MISSIONS

Civilian intelligence community (IC) element	Mission
Central Intelligence Agency (CIA)	Collects, analyzes, evaluates, and disseminates foreign intelligence to assist the President and senior U.S. government policymakers in making decisions relating to national security.
Department of Energy Office of Intelligence and Counterintelligence (DOE IN)	Provides expert scientific, technical, analytic, and research capabilities to other agencies in the IC and participates in formulating intelligence collection, analysis, and information relative to foreign energy matters.
Department of Homeland Security Office of Intelligence and Analysis (DHS I&A)	Equips DHS, other IC elements, departments, state, local, tribal, territorial, and private sector partners with the intelligence and information needed to keep the homeland safe, secure, and resilient.
Department of Justice (DOJ), Drug Enforcement Administration Office of National Security Intelligence (DEA NN)	Facilitates intelligence coordination and information sharing with other members of the IC and leverages its global law enforcement drug intelligence assets to enhance efforts to protect national security, combat global terrorism, and facilitate IC support to DEA's law enforcement mission.
Department of State Bureau of Intelligence and Research (State INR)	Ensures that well-informed and independent analysis informs foreign policy decisions and that intelligence and counterintelligence activities support America's foreign policy.
Department of the Treasury Office of Intelligence and	Receives, analyzes, collates, and disseminates intelligence and counterintelligence information related to the operations and responsibilities of the entire Treasury Department. Publishes analytic products and intelligence information reports for senior leaders at Treasury and

Civilian intelligence community (IC) element	Mission
Analysis (Treasury OIA)	other policymakers and intelligence consumers throughout the government.
DOJ Federal Bureau of Investigation (FBI)	Protects and defends against terrorist and foreign intelligence threats, upholds and enforces the criminal laws of the United States, and provides leadership and criminal justice services to federal, state, municipal, and international agencies and partners.
Office of the Director of National Intelligence (ODNI)	Serves as head of the IC; acts as the principal adviser to the President, National Security Council, and the Homeland Security Council for intelligence matters related to national security; and develops and ensures the execution of an annual budget for the National Intelligence Program based on budget proposals provided by the IC elements.

Source: GAO analysis of civilian IC elements' information.

APPENDIX IV. SELECTED OFFICE OF MANAGEMENT AND BUDGET GUIDANCE RELATED TO CONSIDERING AND MITIGATING RISKS

Office of Management and Budget (OMB) guidance	Selected requirements related to closely supporting inherently governmental functions	Selected requirements related to critical functions
Office of Federal Procurement Policy (OFPP), Management Oversight of Service Contracting, OFPP Policy Letter No. 93-1 (Reissued) (May 18, 1994)	Agency officials must provide an enhanced degree of management controls and oversight when contracting for functions that closely support the performance of inherently governmental functions.	Not applicable
OMB Memorandum, Managing the Multisector	Not applicable	As part of determining whether it is appropriate to use contractors, fill critical

(Continued)

Office of Management and Budget (OMB) guidance	Selected requirements related to closely supporting inherently governmental functions	Selected requirements related to critical functions
Workforce, M-09-26 (July 29, 2009)		functions only with government personnel to the extent required by the agency to maintain control of its mission and operations and by either government or contract personnel once the agency has sufficient internal capability to control its mission and operations.
OFPP Memorandum, Service Contract Inventories (November 5, 2010); OFPP Memorandum, Service Contract Inventories (December 19, 2011)	Beginning with the fiscal year 2012 service contract inventory submissions, identify which contracts include services that are predominantly for functions closely associated to inherently governmental work. Analyze the inventory to ensure the agency is giving special management attention to functions that are closely associated with inherently governmental functions.	Beginning with the fiscal year 2012 service contract inventory submissions, identify which contracts include services that are predominantly for functions that are critical. Analyze the inventory to ensure that the agency is not using contractor employees to perform critical functions in such a way that could affect the ability of the agency to maintain control of its mission and operations.
OFPP Policy Letter 11-01: Performance of Inherently Governmental and Critical Functions (76 Fed. Reg. 56227, September 12, 2011)	Limit or guide a contractor's exercise of discretion and retain control of government operations. Assign a sufficient number of qualified government employees,	Identify agency's critical functions. Ensure that government personnel perform and/or manage critical functions to the extent necessary for the agency to operate effectively and maintain

Office of Management and Budget (OMB) guidance	Selected requirements related to closely supporting inherently governmental functions	Selected requirements related to critical functions
	with expertise to administer or perform the work, to give special management attention to the contractor's activities.	control of its mission and operations.

Source: GAO analysis of OMB guidance.

APPENDIX V. INTELLIGENCE COMMUNITY CORE CONTRACT PERSONNEL DEFINITIONS AND ASSOCIATED MAJOR CHANGES BY FISCAL YEAR

Fiscal year	Core contract personnel definition	Summary of major changes from prior fiscal year
2007	Contracts that provide direct support to core intelligence community (IC) mission areas such as collection activities and operations; intelligence analysis and production; basic and applied technology research and development; acquisition and program management; and/or management and administrative support to these functions. Also, these employees are functionally indistinguishable from U.S. government personnel whose mission they support. Consulting contractors are to be included when they provide primarily intellectual products or services.	N/A
2008	Individuals employed by a private or independent contractor to provide analytical, technical, managerial, and/or administrative support to: (1)	From contracts that provide "direct support" to individuals that "support." Removes "such as" for

(Contiuned)

Fiscal year	Core contract personnel definition	Summary of major changes from prior fiscal year
	intelligence collection activities and operations; (2) intelligence analysis and production; (3) basic and applied technology research and development; (4) acquisition and program management; (5) enterprise information technology; and (6) ongoing operations and maintenance in support of a particular product; and/or support the general management and administration of an IC agency or element.	mission areas and names six core IC mission areas. Adds "enterprise information technology" and "operations and maintenance" as mission areas not previously listed. From "management and administrative support to these functions" to "support the general management and administration of an IC agency or element." Removes that the "employees are functionally indistinguishable from U.S. government personnel whose mission they support."
2009	Personnel that provide only direct support to core IC mission areas that include: (1) collection activities and operations (technical and human intelligence); (2) intelligence analysis and production; (3) basic and applied technology research and development; (4) acquisition and program management; (5) enterprise information technology; and (6) management or administrative support to these functions. Also, these employees are functionally indistinguishable from U.S. government personnel whose mission they support.	From individuals that "support" to personnel that provide "only direct support." Specifies technical and human intelligence for collection activities and operations. Reverts from "support the general management and administration of an IC agency or element" to "management or administrative support of these functions." Adds back in that the "employees are functionally indistinguishable from U.S. government personnel whose mission they support" but does not mention consulting contractors.
2010	Personnel that provide only direct support to core IC mission areas that include: (1) collection activities and	No definitional change. Guidance includes that personnel performing certain

Civilian Intelligence Community 49

Fiscal year	Core contract personnel definition	Summary of major changes from prior fiscal year
	operations (technical and human intelligence), (2) intelligence analysis and production, (3) basic and applied technology research and development, (4) acquisition and program management, (5) enterprise information technology, and (6) management or administrative support to these functions. Also, these employees are functionally indistinguishable from U.S. government personnel whose mission they support.	administrative support, training support, information technology services, and operations and maintenance will either be included or excluded depending on the types of services they provide.
2011	Personnel that provide only direct support to core IC mission areas that include: (1) collection activities and operations (technical and human intelligence), (2) intelligence analysis and production, (3) basic and applied technology research and development, (4) acquisition and program management, (5) enterprise information technology, and (6) management or administrative support to these functions.	Revision to "substantive work products may be incorporated in and/or indistinguishable from those of U.S. government personnel." Guidance further refines the inclusion or exclusion of personnel performing certain administrative support, information technology services, and operations and maintenance.

Source: GAO analysis of IC Chief Human Capital Officer information.

End Notes

[1] Federal Acquisition Regulation (FAR) § 7.503(c) includes a list of functions that are considered to be inherently governmental.

[2] Functions closely associated with the performance of inherently governmental functions are not considered inherently governmental, but may approach being in that category because of the nature of the function, the manner in which the contractor performs the contract, or the manner in which the government administers contractor performance. FAR § 7.503(d).

[3] See generally FAR § 37.114(b), which requires agencies to provide special management attention to contracts for services that require the contractor to provide advice, opinions, recommendations, ideas, reports, analyses, or other work products, as they have the potential for influencing the authority, accountability, and responsibilities of government officials.

[4] GAO, Managing Service Contracts: Recent Efforts to Address Associated Risks Can Be Further Enhanced, GAO-12-87 (Washington, D.C.: Dec. 7, 2011); Contingency Contracting:

Improvements Needed in Management of Contractors Supporting Contract and Grant Administration in Iraq and Afghanistan, GAO-10-357 (Washington, D.C.: Apr. 12, 2010); Defense Acquisitions: Further Actions Needed to Address Weaknesses in DOD's Management of Professional and Management Support Contracts, GAO-10-39 (Washington, D.C.: Nov. 20, 2009); and Department of Homeland Security: Improved Assessment and Oversight Needed to Manage Risk of Contracting for Selected Services, GAO-07-990 (Washington, D.C.: Sept. 17, 2007).

[5] DEA NN and FBI are components of the Department of Justice (DOJ).

[6] For the purposes of this report, a contract record corresponds to one row of data in an element's submission to the inventory for a particular fiscal year. One contract record can represent a contract, a purchase order, or multiple contracts. In addition, multiple contract records can constitute one contract or purchase order. The number of contract records we reviewed was a random sample of the contracts across all eight civilian IC elements and therefore cannot be used to determine the number of contracts for any individual civilian IC element or the civilian IC elements as a whole.

[7] Our sample was not generalizable because two of the civilian IC elements removed certain records from the universe of records available for random selection. In addition, after making our initial random selection, we worked with several civilian IC elements to remove and replace certain records from our selection if they identified sensitivity concerns or could not readily locate relevant documents.

[8] OFPP Policy Letter 11-01, Performance of Inherently Governmental and Critical Functions (Sept. 12, 2011); OMB M-09-26, Managing the Multisector Workforce (July 29, 2009); OFPP Memorandum for Chief Acquisition Officers and Senior Procurement Executives, Service Contract Inventories (Nov. 5, 2010); and OFPP Memorandum for Chief Acquisition Officers and Senior Procurement Executives, Service Contract Inventories (Dec. 19, 2011).

[9] GAO, A Model of Strategic Human Capital Management, GAO-02-373SP (Washington, D.C.: Mar. 15, 2002).

[10] The National Intelligence Program, overseen by ODNI, provides the resources needed to develop and maintain intelligence capabilities that support national priorities. Pub. L. No. 108-458, § 1011.

[11] The eight Department of Defense IC elements that were not within the scope of our review were Air Force Intelligence, Surveillance and Reconnaissance; Army Military Intelligence; the Defense Intelligence Agency; Marine Corps Intelligence; the National Geospatial-Intelligence Agency; the National Reconnaissance Office; the National Security Agency; and Naval Intelligence. We also did not include DHS's Coast Guard Intelligence and Criminal Investigations in our review because the Coast Guard is considered a military organization.

[12] The different data fields include information such as the name of the contractor, amount of funds obligated in a fiscal year, number of total direct labor hours, number of contractor FTEs, and reason for using a contractor to perform the service. The number and types of data fields available vary by fiscal year.

[13] Intelligence Authorization Act for Fiscal Year 2010, Pub. L. No. 111-259, § 305(a).

[14] OFPP Policy Letter 92-1, Inherently Governmental Functions (Sept. 23, 1992 [Rescinded]); OFPP Policy Letter 93-1, Management Oversight of Service Contracting (May 18, 1994).

[15] FAR § 37.114(b).

[16] Certain civilian IC elements have the authority to hire personal services contractors. The FAR does not explicitly prohibit these contractors from performing inherently governmental functions.

[17] OMB M-09-26 (July 29, 2009); GAO-02-373SP.

[18] GAO, Human Capital: A Self-Assessment Checklist for Agency Leaders, GAO/OCG-00-14G (Washington, D.C.: September 2000).

[19] GAO, Human Capital: Additional Steps Needed to Help Determine the Right Size and Composition of DOD's Total Workforce, GAO-13-470 (Washington, D.C.: May 29, 2013).

[20] OFPP Memorandum, Service Contract Inventories (Nov. 5, 2010); OFPP Memorandum, Service Contract Inventories (Dec. 19, 2011).

[21] GAO, Defense Acquisitions: Continued Management Attention Needed to Enhance Use and Review of DOD's Inventory of Contracted Services, GAO-13-491 (Washington, D.C.: May 23, 2013); Civilian Service Contract Inventories: Opportunities Exist to Improve Agency Reporting and Review Efforts, GAO-12-1007 (Washington, D.C.: Sept. 27, 2012); and Sourcing Policy: Initial Agency Efforts to Balance the Government to Contractor Mix in the Multisector Workforce, GAO-10-744T (Washington, D.C.: May 20, 2010).

[22] 31 U.S.C. § 501, note, and 10 U.S.C. § 2330a(a).

[23] GAO-12-1007.

[24] GAO-13-491.

[25] Office of Management and Budget, Guidelines for Ensuring and Maximizing the Quality, Objectivity, Utility, and Integrity of Information Disseminated by Federal Agencies. 67 Fed. Reg. 8452 (Feb. 22, 2002).

[26] Internal controls should provide reasonable assurance that the objectives of the agency are being achieved according to the following categories: effectiveness and efficiency of operations including the use of the entity's resources; reliability of financial reporting, including reports on budget execution, financial statements, and other reports for internal and external use; and compliance with applicable laws and regulations. Internal controls may vary by agency due to a number of factors, such as the size and complexity of the organization. Examples of internal control activities include reviews by management, accurate and timely recording of transactions, and appropriate documentation of transactions and internal control. GAO, Standards for Internal Control in the Federal Government, GAO/AIMD-00-21.3.1 (Washington, D.C.: November 1999).

[27] We were unable to determine the full magnitude of obligations not included in the inventory because we did not have a way to identify all contracts not reported by the civilian IC elements.

[28] GAO/AIMD-00-21.3.1.

[29] Office of Management and Budget, Guidelines for Ensuring and Maximizing the Quality, Objectivity, Utility, and Integrity of Information Disseminated by Federal Agencies. 67 Fed. Reg. 8452 (Feb. 22, 2002).

[30] The IC CHCO core contract personnel inventory guidance instructs the elements to complete the budget category data field by reporting where the funding for the contract is assigned according to the Congressional Budget Justification Books.

[31] GAO-12-87.

[32] OMB M-09-26 (July 29, 2009); GAO-02-373SP; and GAO, Human Capital: A Self-Assessment Checklist for Agency Leaders, GAO/OCG-00-14G (Washington, D.C.: September 2000).

[33] OMB M-09-26 (July 29, 2009).

[34] OFPP, Service Contract Inventories (Nov. 5, 2010).

[35] DEA NN and FBI are components of the Department of Justice (DOJ).

[36] OFPP Policy Letter 11-01, Performance of Inherently Governmental and Critical Functions (Sept. 12, 2011).

[37] OMB M-09-26, Managing the Multisector Workforce (July 29, 2009) and GAO, A Model of Strategic Human Capital Management, GAO-02-373SP (Washington, D.C.: Mar. 15, 2002).

[38] OFPP Memorandum for Chief Acquisition Officers and Senior Procurement Executives, Service Contract Inventories (Nov. 5, 2010); and OFPP Memorandum for Chief Acquisition Officers and Senior Procurement Executives, Service Contract Inventories, (Dec. 19, 2011).

[39] The eight civilian IC elements covered by our review are the Central Intelligence Agency (CIA), the Department of Energy's Office of Intelligence and Counterintelligence (DOE IN), Department of Homeland Security's Office of Intelligence and Analysis (DHS I&A), Department of State's Bureau of Intelligence and Research (State INR), Department of the Treasury's Office of Intelligence and Analysis (Treasury OIA), Drug Enforcement

Administration's Office of National Security Intelligence (DEA NN), Federal Bureau of Investigation (FBI), and Office of the Director of National Intelligence (ODNI).

[40] We identified the budget category as related to our intended purposes because IC CHCO uses the data field in its briefings to Congress to provide information on the functions performed by core contract personnel.

[41] Government auditing standards require that auditors assess the sufficiency and appropriateness of computer-processed information. According to GAO standards for assessing the reliability of computer-processed data, reliability means that data are reasonably complete, accurate, consistent, meet the audit's intended purposes, and are not subject to inappropriate alteration. For more information about GAO's data reliability standards, see GAO, Applied Research and Methods: Assessing the Reliability of Computer-Processed Data, GAO-09-680G (Washington, D.C.: July 2009).

[42] IC CHCO conducted a pilot for the inventory in fiscal year 2006.

[43] For the purposes of this report, a contract record corresponds to one row of data in an element's submission to the inventory for a particular fiscal year. One contract record can represent a contract, a purchase order, or multiple contracts. In addition, multiple contract records can constitute one contract or purchase order. The number of contract records we reviewed was a random sample of the contracts across all eight civilian IC elements and therefore cannot be used to determine the number of contracts for any individual civilian IC element or the civilian IC elements as a whole.

[44] Our sample was not generalizable because two of the civilian IC elements removed certain records from the universe of records available for random selection. In addition, after making our initial random selection, we worked with several civilian IC elements to remove and replace certain records from our selection if they identified sensitivity concerns or could not readily locate relevant documents.

[45] While we initially identified records in which the information in relevant documents appeared to contradict the information reported, we did not break out this group for the purposes of this analysis for two key reasons. First, an element may calculate the number of FTEs using methods that cannot be verified through documents, such as counting the number of contract personnel working on a particular date or including the number of contractor vacancies in the number reported. In addition, elements may not have provided all relevant documents that would allow us to validate the information reported.

In: Contractors in the Civilian Intelligence ... ISBN: 978-1-63321-160-5
Editor: Maxwell Gibbs © 2014 Nova Science Publishers, Inc.

Chapter 2

STATEMENT OF STEPHANIE O'SULLIVAN, PRINCIPAL DEPUTY DIRECTOR, OFFICE OF THE DIRECTOR OF NATIONAL INTELLIGENCE. HEARING ON " THE INTELLIGENCE COMMUNITY: KEEPING WATCH OVER ITS CONTRACTOR WORKFORCE"[*]

INTRODUCTION

Chairman Carper and Ranking Member Coburn, thank you for the invitation to testify today on the ODNI's oversight and monitoring of Intelligence Community (IC) core contract personnel and their role. I appreciate the Committee's interest in this issue. I trust the information provided to you today will strengthen your confidence in the efforts of the IC leadership to manage and oversee this critical component of our combined workforce.

In addition to addressing the specific questions in your invitation letter regarding the Government Accountability Office's (GAO) recent report on IC core contract personnel, I will provide the Committee with some background

---

[*] This is an edited, reformatted and augmented version of a statement prepared for a hearing originally scheduled to be held on February 13, 2014 before the Senate Homeland Security and Governmental Affairs Committee.

on why core contract personnel have been and are an important part of our workforce.

Furthermore, I will address our broader strategic workforce planning efforts, which includes oversight of IC core contract personnel.

THE GROWTH OF CORE CONTRACT PERSONNEL AND WHY WE USE THEM

The IC workforce is composed of three distinct elements: civilian United States Government (USG) personnel, members of the armed forces, and core contract personnel. As a result of the Cold War peace dividend, the IC was significantly downsized throughout the 1990s. Limits on hiring resulted in reductions in the number of analysts, operators, scientists, and support personnel across the Community. There was a degradation of the Community's capabilities as older, more experienced employees retired and far fewer employees were hired to take their place. During these years the IC was encouraged to "outsource" as much as possible, especially in the area of information technology support.

The terrorist attacks of September 11, 2001 and ensuing conflicts caused an abrupt shift. Expertise was needed quickly to meet rapidly evolving mission demands. To meet these emerging requirements, the IC leveraged contract personnel to provide the requisite skills and experience. Congressionally-imposed civilian personnel ceilings and emergency supplemental funding also drove increased reliance on contract personnel. Given the unplanned and potentially fluctuating nature of Overseas Contingency Operations funding, contract personnel were better suited for many tasks. In addition, contract personnel brought unique skills in critical languages, terrorism analysis, cyber, and a host of other areas where there was inadequate expertise in our Community. We have, however, turned the corner and for the past several years have been reducing the number of core contract personnel across the IC, both in numbers and costs. Despite these reductions, core contract personnel have now become an integral part of the IC workforce. We could not perform our mission without them. At the same time that the IC's use of contract personnel was expanding during the last decade, the IC hired thousands of new government employees, and trained and deployed them as quickly as possible. I would like to stress this point: government civilians are the heart of our workforce. Contract personnel play an important role in our workforce (as do military personnel), and we need to identify, on a strategic level, the activities and functions that they will perform. But this is secondary to performing a much more important strategic level evaluation of the size of the civilian workforce, the roles and activities that it performs, how it is trained and managed, and so forth. For example, I can make investments, in terms of training and career development, in my civilian and military workforces that I cannot make with the contract workforce. Contract personnel support and supplement the civilian and military workforce, but they do not perform our most important jobs and missions. Often they provide unique but perishable skills that would be costly to replicate in our government workforce.

The IC continues to proactively evaluate the role of contract personnel, taking into consideration the mission, expertise required, and cost. As a result, the IC has and continues to reduce core contract personnel in many areas and refine the balance with the other components of the IC workforce. This is a dynamic process that will continue.

DEFINING "CORE CONTRACT PERSONNEL" AND WHAT THEY DO

Contract personnel provide a broad spectrum of services, as permitted by law and regulation. As a general matter, the use of contract personnel is governed primarily by the Federal Acquisition Regulation. The Office of Management and Budget (OMB) and the Federal Activities Inventory Reform Act also provide guidance regarding the performance of inherently governmental activities.

The IC defines "core contract personnel" as those who support government civilian and military members by providing direct technical and intellectual expertise, or administrative assistance. Core contract personnel typically work alongside of and are integrated with USG civilian and military personnel, and perform staff-like functions. They provide unique expertise, surge capacity, cost-effective services and support, and services of limited duration. These attributes make contract personnel an extremely flexible part of our workforce. Core contract personnel serve side-by-side with our government civilians and military personnel, and in some cases have given their lives for this country alongside their government colleagues. Two IC contract personnel were among the nine people killed during a terrorist attack on a CIA facility located near the eastern Afghan city of Khost in December

2009, and two IC contract personnel lost their lives during the attack on US diplomatic facilities in Benghazi, Libya, in September 2012.

Core contract personnel do not produce specific commodities such as a satellite or information systems, nor do they provide ongoing operations and maintenance in support of that product. (Those are industrial contractors.) Core contract personnel also do not provide what are considered commercially available services such as food, facilities maintenance, or janitorial services as defined by OMB Circular A-76 (Revised 2003).

Core contract personnel hold clearances and have access to classified information in the performance of intelligence activities, including collection, analysis, information technology, training, and education. As such, they are required to follow the same laws, policies, and regulations as government employees and military personnel for access to and the handling of classified information.

Core contract personnel may not and do not perform inherently governmental functions. Decisions regarding priorities, strategic direction, or commitment of resources always remain with government officials. I believe the IC's use of core contract personnel, since 9/11 and before, is appropriate and justified, and we take oversight of the contract workforce seriously.

Strengthening the IC Workforce and Oversight of Core Contract Personnel

As I noted earlier, the IC has been focused on growing and strengthening its civilian workforce for more than a decade. Significant investments have been made to recruit, train, develop, and deploy Community personnel since 9/11. In many important areas, the IC needs people with special skills that cannot be readily acquired through hiring on the open market and that take many years to develop.

Therefore, the IC is building its own hiring pipelines in areas such as cyber and cybersecurity; foreign language; and science, technology, engineering, and mathematics. Initiatives such as the National Security Agency/Department of Homeland Security Centers of Academic Excellence Program in Information Assurance, the National Security Education Program, and other similar programs have been designed to develop a pool of educated and capable individuals with mission critical skills. In addition, IC elements have strong internship and cooperative education programs in these areas which also continue to attract numbers of exceptional applicants and provide a pipeline to permanent employment.

The IC leadership closely monitors the results of the annual IC Employee Climate Survey to track employee satisfaction and retention. The survey, which has been administered annually since 2006, provides direct feedback on employee perceptions and perspectives. While the IC continues to experience relatively low attrition rates, the Director of National Intelligence (DNI) holds heads of IC elements accountable for taking action in areas where employees indicate valid concerns. The IC has been recognized by the Partnership for Public Service as one of the top five best places to work in the federal government for the last three years and in the top ten the two years prior. However, the last several years have presented challenges, including furloughs, sequestration, and pay freezes, that may negatively affect our ability to hire and retain government personnel.

Strategic workforce planning is the foundation of all of our human capital initiatives, and core contract personnel are included in our planning. We must have the capability - as a community - to project future mission-critical skill requirements; compare current inventories of civilian, military and core contract personnel capabilities against those requirements; and develop effective plans to close critical skill gaps.

Achieving the right balance among government civilians, military, and core contract personnel is critical to our ability to meet the demands of our mission. To this end, we have:

- Integrated personnel planning into the budget process. Every National Intelligence Program Congressional Budget Justification Book includes a Workforce Overview and graphical displays showing the balance between government personnel (civilian and military) and contract support; and
- Required IC elements to brief their Human Capital Employment Plans to the IC Chief Human Capital Office. These strategic workforce plans address all three workforce components. They provide an overview and profile of each IC element's workforce, assessment of critical skills and workforce mix, and human capital priorities going forward.

During this time we have also taken a number of actions to improve our oversight and management of IC core contract personnel. In 2006, the ODNI conducted its first inventory of core contract personnel directly supporting the

IC's mission. This year we will conduct our eighth inventory and will continue to refine and improve our methodology. Specifically, we will require each IC element to provide a written explanation of the methodology used to identify and calculate the values for the data points. The IC elements will be asked to describe the methodology used to obtain, determine, and validate the value for the number of hours to determine a Full Time Equivalent. We also ask respondents to include any factors that may create variations in value, calculations, etc. ODNI reviews and analyzes each IC element's submissions, which is followed by a briefing to OMB that includes the results and ODNI's analysis of the inventory submissions.

In addition, any changes or clarification to the definitions are coordinated with OMB to ensure we adhere to OMB guidance.

As GAO has noted, there have been challenges associated with conducting the inventory, which was one of the first of its kind in the Federal government. IC elements vary in their ability to capture core contract data in an efficient and timely manner. For example, some elements compile the data manually, and all elements depend on timely and accurate contractor invoice submittals. However, the IC continues to improve the capture and understanding of data on its core contract personnel. As a result, over the years we have highlighted to OMB and Congress major adjustments and revisions of inventory data that affected the count of previous years. We expect that further improvements in "data capture" will make our information more reliable.

The DNI approved Intelligence Community Directive (ICD) 612 on October 30, 2009 to guide the use of core contract personnel. Among its key provisions, this Directive:

- Reaffirms the prohibition on the use of core contract personnel to perform inherently governmental activities;
- Generally describes the circumstances in which core contract personnel may be employed to support IC missions and functions;
- Beginning in FY 2011, requires IC elements to determine, review, and evaluate the actual and projected number and uses of core contract personnel in support of their intelligence missions;
- Makes permanent the annual inventory of IC core contract personnel, first initiated in June 2006; and
- Provides a refined definition of core contract personnel to ensure that IC elements can accurately conduct that inventory.

Overall, the ODNI has made great strides in overseeing the use of IC core contract personnel and will continue to refine our management of them, to include an assessment of the costs of these contracts. Generally we are finding that the rates on the new competitive contracts are substantially lower than we had been paying on the predecessor efforts. Because of the contraction in budgets, contractors are motivated to reduce costs. This is going on in both their indirect rates but even in the salaries being paid to the employees. In fact, some contractor employees are now being paid less than they were a few years back. As agencies cut Full-Time Equivalents (FTEs), the result is a larger supply of labor which drives down labor costs. We will continue to monitor this to ensure we do not go too far and lose the expertise we are paying for in exchange for these lower costs.

Implementation of the Office of Federal Procurement Policy's (OFPP) Policy Letter 11-01, "Performance of Inherently Governmental and Critical Functions," creates a single definition for the term "inherently governmental function," reinforces the special management responsibilities that agencies use ifo! relying on contract personnel to perform work that is closely associated with an inherently governmental function, establishes criteria to identify critical functions and positions that should only be performed by Federal employees, and provides guidance to improve management of functions that are inherently governmental or critical.

Implementation of this policy letter is a shared responsibility across the IC acquisition, human capital, and financial management communities. Because the IC has been closely reviewing its core contract personnel workforce for several years, IC elements have conducted reviews of the functions and activities of their core contract workforces, and have taken steps to remedy situations where there was over-reliance on core contract personnel in tasks closely associated with inherently governmental functions.

The policy letter introduces a new category, "critical function," to ensure agencies have sufficient internal capability to maintain control over functions that are core to their mission and operations. Contract personnel may perform critical functions as long as the government has the internal capacity to manage its work and that of its contract personnel. We believe our "core contract personnel" practices are responsive to the policy letter's guidance, and we are reviewing the details carefully to consider where we may need to make additional refinements to our policies to best implement this policy letter across the IC.

GAO Recommendations

GAO recommended that the IC Chief Human Capital Office (CHCO) develop a plan to enhance internal controls for compiling annual Core Contract Personnel Inventory data, specify limitations of the data, and describe the methodologies used. The IC CHCO, in coordination with the IC Chief Financial Officer, added a new section to the FY 2015 Core Contract Personnel Inventory data call that supports this request. The new section requires each IC element to provide a written response on the methodology used to identify and calculate the values for the data points submitted and describe the methodology used to obtain, determine, and populate the value for the number of contract personnel hours used to determine a FTE. IC agencies will now also identify limitations that influence variations in value, calculations, etc. These changes will bring greater transparency to the IC's data on core contract personnel.

GAO also recommended that the IC develop guidance to augment the findings of OFPP Policy Letter 11-01. As noted above, we are working closely across the IC to ensure we are in line with the policy letter. The IC CHCO has recently issued guidance in the new core contract personnel inventory data call that requests IC elements describe steps taken to ensure compliance with this Policy Letter.

GAO also recommended that ODNI examine and revise lCD 612 and adjust the provision governing strategic workforce planning to require the IC elements to identify their assessments of the appropriate mix of government and contract personnel. The revision of this lCD is the highest policy priority for the IC CHCO and will be initiated this year.

ODNI has directed the IC elements to continue to determine, review, and evaluate the actual and projected number and uses of core contract personnel in workforce planning. As I mentioned earlier, the appropriate workforce mix is not a static percentage, and may vary considerably across the IC elements and from year to year. The optimal mix of the workforce is determined based on an analysis of each IC element's mission needs. Funding, positions, critical skill needs, and mission requirements are all key determinants. Other factors to consider are the length of time involved in hiring the government employee, and whether the function is intended for the long-term. In addition, each IC element head has the responsibility to ensure the element has sufficient staff with trained government contract management personnel to oversee these core contract personnel.

GAO recommended that ODNI assess options for modifying the core contract personnel inventory to provide better insights into functions performed by core contract personnel if there are multiple services provided under a contract. While the IC CHCO is committed to providing more reliable and transparent data on core contract personnel, we assess that the effort to develop the capability to track this level of information on every individual contract would be time and cost prohibitive. It also would be of minimal value for workforce planning, since the inventory focuses solely on the previous year's contract data. However, as we update lCD 612, we will consider changes that would facilitate the generation of better data.

Another GAO recommendation is for each IC element to capture data on individual contracts, identifying the number of core contract personnel considered "critical" or "closely related." While there is no reporting requirement for these data in OFPP Policy Letter 11-01, we will assess the viability of capturing this level of information to include references to "critical" and "closely related" functions during the revision of lCD 612.

MOVING FORWARD

To meet today' s national security threats, we need a workforce that is second to none, and this workforce will include core contract personnel. We will continue to manage this segment of our workforce in a manner that is consistent with law, regulation, our budgetary restrictions, and our mission requirements to protect our country. I believe that the IC's use of core contract personnel has been consistent with these requirements and in the best interests of the taxpayers.

Thank you, I look forward to answering your questions.

INDEX

#

9/11, 56

A

access, 56
accountability, 5, 9, 49
accounting, 18
administrative support, 5, 14, 47, 48, 49
Afghanistan, 50
agencies, 5, 6, 8, 9, 11, 12, 15, 22, 25, 26, 27, 28, 29, 30, 33, 44, 45, 49, 59, 60
Air Force, 50
armed forces, 54
assessment, 6, 9, 14, 15, 30, 31, 35, 57, 59
assets, 44
Attorney General, 31
audit, 7, 17, 36, 37, 52
authority, 2, 3, 9, 49, 50

B

benefits, 5
budget line, 40

C

career development, 55
category a, 52
category b, 49
category d, 21, 41, 42, 51
challenges, 12, 17, 19, 20, 57, 58
CIA, 2, 3, 4, 6, 24, 25, 26, 30, 32, 33, 34, 40, 44, 51, 55
civilian IC elements, vii, 1, 2, 3, 4, 6, 7, 8, 11, 13, 16, 18, 19, 20, 21, 22, 23, 24, 26, 27, 28, 29, 30, 31, 33, 34, 35, 36, 37, 38, 39, 40, 41, 42, 45, 50, 51, 52
clarity, 15
Coast Guard, 50
coding, 23, 29, 43
Cold War, 54
commercial, 5
community(s), 2, 4, 34, 36, 44, 45, 47, 57, 59
competition, 40
complexity, 51
compliance, 51, 60
computer, 52
Congress, 2, 5, 9, 13, 14, 15, 17, 20, 21, 22, 29, 32, 35, 41, 52, 58
consulting, 48
consumers, 45
contract records, vii, 2, 3, 50, 52
coordination, 31, 32, 44, 60
cost, 2, 3, 13, 27, 30, 55, 61
cybersecurity, 56

Index

D

data collection, 14, 29, 33
DEA, 3, 5, 6, 11, 34, 44, 50, 51, 52
degradation, 54
Department of Defense, 3, 6, 50
Department of Energy, 3, 5, 34, 44, 51
Department of Homeland Security, 3, 4, 34, 44, 50, 51, 56
Department of Justice, 3, 44, 50, 51
Department of the Treasury, 4, 5, 34, 44, 51
DHS, 3, 4, 6, 25, 26, 32, 34, 44, 50, 51
disclosure, 6, 36
DOJ, 3, 11, 26, 30, 32, 33, 44, 45, 50, 51
draft, 32, 34
Drug Enforcement Administration, 3, 5, 34, 44, 52

E

education, 56
emergency, 54
employees, 5, 10, 25, 46, 47, 48, 49, 54, 56, 57, 59
employment, 27, 57
energy, 44
enforcement, 44
engineering, 21, 56
evidence, 3, 7, 11, 20, 22, 36
exclusion, 18, 49
execution, 9, 45, 51
executive branch, 12
exercise, 46
expertise, 3, 5, 7, 10, 20, 21, 22, 23, 24, 28, 34, 37, 40, 43, 47, 54, 55, 59

F

Federal Bureau of Investigation (FBI), 4, 5, 6, 34, 45, 50, 51, 52
federal government, 4, 5, 8, 51, 57
federal law, 11
financial, 22, 51, 59
fiscal year 2009, 13, 14, 15, 16
flexibility, 5
food, 56
foreign intelligence, 44, 45
foreign language, 56
foreign policy, 44
funding, 22, 37, 41, 51, 54
funds, 18, 39, 50

G

GAO, vii, 1, 2, 3, 8, 10, 35, 40, 45, 47, 49, 50, 51, 52, 53, 58, 60, 61
government personnel, vii, 1, 5, 11, 27, 33, 46, 47, 48, 49, 57
government policy, 44
guidance, 2, 3, 6, 7, 9, 11, 12, 14, 17, 18, 19, 21, 22, 23, 24, 25, 26, 27, 28, 29, 30, 31, 32, 34, 35, 37, 38, 41, 42, 43, 45, 46, 47, 51, 55, 58, 59, 60
guidelines, 15, 16, 22, 30

H

hiring, 54, 56, 60
host, 54
human, 7, 9, 20, 21, 26, 27, 35, 48, 49, 57, 59
human capital, 7, 20, 21, 26, 27, 35, 57, 59

I

improvements, 14, 15, 58
individuals, 47, 48, 56
information sharing, 44
information technology, 2, 14, 15, 20, 21, 22, 48, 49, 54, 56
intelligence, 2, 4, 5, 8, 30, 34, 36, 44, 45, 47, 48, 49, 50, 56, 58
intelligence community, 2, 4, 34, 36, 44, 45, 47
Intelligence Reform and Terrorism Prevention Act, 8
internal controls, 17, 30, 31, 32, 60
internship, 56

investments, 55, 56
Iraq, 50
issues, 13, 17

J

justification, 40

L

languages, 54
law enforcement, 44
laws, 11, 45, 51, 56
laws and regulations, 11, 51
lead, 18
leadership, 26, 45, 53, 57
light, 17

M

magnitude, 40, 41, 51
majority, 38
management, 2, 5, 9, 15, 17, 20, 21, 22, 25, 26, 28, 29, 30, 33, 45, 46, 47, 48, 49, 51, 57, 59, 60
Marine Corps, 50
mathematics, 56
matter, 55
methodology, 7, 16, 18, 19, 20, 35, 40, 58, 60
military, 8, 9, 22, 24, 50, 55, 56, 57
mission(s), 5, 8, 10, 11, 12, 14, 24, 25, 26, 27, 28, 29, 30, 33, 43, 44, 46, 47, 48, 49, 54, 55, 56, 57, 58, 59, 60, 61
modifications, 39

N

national security, 44, 45, 61
National Security Agency, 50, 56
National Security Council, 8, 45

O

officials, vii, 2, 6, 7, 9, 14, 15, 16, 17, 18, 19, 20, 22, 23, 26, 27, 28, 29, 31, 35, 36, 37, 38, 39, 40, 41, 42, 43, 45, 49, 56
Office of Management and Budget (OMB), 4, 7, 9, 11, 12, 15, 16, 22, 26, 27, 30, 32, 35, 45, 46, 47, 50, 51, 55, 56, 58
operations, 10, 11, 12, 17, 21, 22, 27, 29, 30, 33, 44, 46, 47, 48, 49, 51, 56, 59
oversight, vii, 1, 5, 9, 12, 26, 28, 31, 33, 45, 53, 54, 56, 57

P

peace, 54
personnel costs, 9, 16
personnel inventory data, vii, 1
pipeline, 57
policy, 5, 9, 11, 12, 22, 25, 26, 30, 32, 35, 44, 59, 60
policymakers, 45
preparation, 20
President, 8, 44, 45
private sector, 44
procurement, 7, 9, 36
project, 23, 57

Q

qualifications, 16

R

recommendations, 2, 12, 32, 49
Reform, 55
regulations, 5, 11, 56
reliability, vii, 1, 2, 6, 13, 14, 15, 17, 19, 29, 34, 37, 42, 51, 52
requirements, 3, 11, 12, 20, 25, 26, 27, 31, 32, 35, 45, 46, 47, 54, 57, 60, 61
resources, 17, 23, 24, 28, 50, 51, 56
response, 9, 14, 22, 23, 28, 42, 43, 60

restrictions, 23, 61
risk(s), 3, 5, 6, 7, 9, 11, 12, 24, 25, 26, 28, 29, 30, 31, 32, 33, 34, 35, 36

S

science, 56
scope, 7, 8, 50
security, 5, 21
security services, 21
Senate, 4, 53
sensitivity, vii, 2, 50, 52
September 11, 5, 54
services, vii, 1, 2, 3, 5, 6, 9, 11, 12, 14, 22, 23, 24, 25, 26, 28, 29, 30, 31, 32, 33, 35, 43, 45, 46, 47, 49, 50, 55, 56, 61
showing, 57
staffing, 23, 24
state(s), 5, 12, 18, 44, 45
strategic planning, 3, 7, 36
stress, 54
subjectivity, 23

T

target, 18, 27, 29, 41
taxpayers, 5, 61
technical assistance, 24
technical comments, 32, 33
technology, 47, 48, 49, 56
territorial, 44

terrorism, 44, 54
terrorist attack, 5, 54, 55
threats, 45, 61
time frame, 26, 30, 31, 32
training, 14, 49, 55, 56
transactions, 17, 51
transparency, 2, 30, 60
Treasury, 2, 4, 5, 6, 26, 30, 31, 32, 33, 34, 44, 45, 51
turnover, 20

U

United, v, 1, 4, 31, 45, 54
United States, v, 1, 4, 31, 45, 54
universe, 50, 52
updating, 26

V

vacancies, 41, 52
variations, 58, 60

W

Washington, 49, 50, 51, 52
workforce, vii, 1, 2, 3, 5, 6, 7, 11, 12, 25, 26, 27, 28, 30, 31, 32, 33, 35, 36, 53, 54, 55, 56, 57, 59, 60, 61